TWO REVIEWS: 50 Scenes in 58 days Is Manic Dynamite

Bukowski meets Henry Miller equals Author Twayne's masterpiece
50 Scenes in 58 days. Strolling through the labyrinth that is the world
of Sigmond, a soap opera has occurred. *50 Scenes in 58 days* is
an unusual twist on telling a tale of trials and tribulations of a unique
writer and his perplexing interactions in Hollywood. Twayne places
his characters in tantalizing roles throughout the real world of Hollywood's
hospitality industry. As you read drama will unfold and Sigmond
will emerge a star on his own big screen. –Liquid City Kendra

Twayne's sexy *Mental Cookbook* is not a cookbook. In his first book, Twayne
takes the reader on a lively tour of pop culture and modern language via figures
of speech and other wordplay as well as basic science, romance and philosophy.

In *50 Scenes in 58 days,* Twayne expounds on being independent and
sticking to writing. He quickly bounces to local popular neighborhoods
where one might seek out in their quest for love -- or as he writes you
quickly find yourself in a bar with a flirty high-fashion debutante.

Playful writing and images of beautiful women: Twayne allows you a peek
at the glamorous side of LA's night life. You'll take a scenic ride through
Los Angeles and enjoy photos complete with images of American Broadcasting
Company's red banners to the newest L.A. Red Line train stations.

50 Scenes in 58 days allows you to wander through L.A. without being there.
Twayne cleverly alternates from describing Hollywood's elderly to reactions
to beautiful women. You never know where he's going to take you, but he
generously leaves you glimpses of real people and a touch of bar wisdom.

50 Scenes is a fast-paced L.A. adventure that will make you smile and wonder about the reality of glamour while it entices you to go on a pub crawl to all the cool bars around L.A. Twayne's life story takes you on a Hollywood trip that goes on and on until the last chapter. As a bonus, *50 Scenes in 58 days'* closing credits read like a movie from The Beach Boys to Zorro and ZZ Top. An intelligent social, poetic commentary, *50 Scenes* will stick in your memories and challenge you to savor the party side of L.A.

Mary Ried – Chicago, IL.
Author, *Pearl Mountain*

50 Scenes
in 58 days

from Ma Jo Ro to a Super singer

A broad view of brightly colored characters
at the most fun places near mountain trails
in the golden state and greater America

<-> An Interactive e-Book: YouTube music links <->

Twayne

 iUniverse®

50 SCENES IN 58 DAYS
FROM MA JO RO TO A SUPER SINGER

iUniverse books may be ordered through booksellers or by contacting:

iUniverse
1663 Liberty Drive
Bloomington, IN 47403
www.iuniverse.com
1-800-Authors (1-800-288-4677)

Because of the dynamic nature of the Internet, any web addresses or links contained in this book may have changed since publication and may no longer be valid. The views expressed in this work are solely those of the author and do not necessarily reflect the views of the publisher, and the publisher hereby disclaims any responsibility for them.

ISBN: 978-1-4917-9232-2 (sc)
ISBN: 978-1-4917-9231-5 (e)

Library of Congress Control Number: 2016904976

Print information available on the last page.

iUniverse rev. date: 10/04/2016

The names in this story are characters in the play
that Shakespeare spoke of as the world stage

Rainbows & waterfalls
PRESENT

Once Upon a Time
In a sunny, happening village of four million . . .

Scene 1: A Soap Opera Is Born . . .

A few doors down from Jimmy Kimmel Live . . .

You Know you've Arrived in Hollywood when
a club owner sees several Actors Showcase
e-mails sent to the show's top actress/creator

and then The Pig blew the Whistle
(which set this story in motion)
when its director off stage
saw a new actor going on
C'est la vie – in the big city. . .

What likely may have evolved was the
prospect of the director's brightest star's mild
interest in such a suave, debonair gentleman

No one ever said the rise to the top
wouldn't have a few slippery boulders –
But now Sig Just Did! . . .And he LIKES It!

/Bright Lights\

Sigmond loves the
Hollywood/Las Palmas Green Light District
where a black leathered, nose-ringed British man
wears a 'Dolly Parton' shirt? No, It's a "Divine" T-shirt!

Empowered by the unempowered –
A Fast Mover who is totally down
with the natives of Hollywood . . .

High on Life and American spirit,
Appreciated Everywhere he goes
(except by owners-managers who like
their superficial {super official} control)

There's a new kid in town on
Hollywood Blvd: Las Palmas to Highland

Meanwhile, back at the ranch (Fred 62),
bright & alert Erin displays classic niceness
(with all-night practicality and charm)

Typical scenario –
 Sitting alone in a bar?
   Then Manifest Love and
    she will come sit beside you
    (right after the guy with the mullet moves over)
    from the Book of Probable Outcomes

P.S. Life in the fast lane will be favorable to you
      if you are favorably beneficial to life

Excuse Siggy now while he grabs 5 hours sleep . . . . .

Scene 2: "(That's) Life In The Big City" . . .

Sig falls in love every 10 minutes OR every ten days – whichever comes first
  {just like an old-fashioned 'Rock Solid' 'Iron Clad' Guarantee ad on TV}
    If blossoming, they're on the radar

Here's How It All Shakes Down –

  "Are You on Meds?"

  "NO! I'm on Stage!" (essentially the same thing) . . .

In a casual social setting
You are Not to act intense
while in delivery (monologuing / speaking)

Conversely, when you ARE on stage
you Must be intense in delivery (passionate / forceful)

Cliff Notes: 1. When you're NOT on stage, don't act like you ARE
            2. If you Are on stage, don't act like you're NOT . . .

      "... And the Wisdom to Know the Difference"
      -- AA (Actors Anonymous)

Now Appearing at HMS Bounty, Jamesons, BJ's Burbank
            (Wilshire, Hollywood, 1st Avenue)

Once a person feels relatively secure, there's little desire
to pick up the redhead at the bus stop – and besides,
there are more fish in the sea than one can manage

Sometimes when Sig feels substantially confident in himself
   THAT's what annoys other people: TMIAO
   (Too Much Information At Once)
   Oh My! Aren't we a sensitive bunch!

Extreme Independence and mental activity is a Virtue
Even if it does make dogs bark, women wary (or Indifferent)
and causes a 12" stream of gasoline to shoot up in the air
only by lifting the nozzle out of its resting place

Sigmond F.T.S.H.
   Fledgling Thespian
   Seasoned Host

Time To Adjust –

After more than 10 years,
   Sig changed his Debit card PIN to someone's birthday . . .
   by the time the new PIN becomes natural for him to remember
   it might be natural for that someone to remember him

Scene 3: Multi-Lingual & Cunni-Lingual . . .

. . . AKA "Soap Opera Digest"

E-Mail - Snail Mail - Tail Mail
                    'sexting'

I'm gonna give you some lovin' until
 your body just "Can't Takes It" No More!
-- Popeye the Sailor Man

415 - 213 - 312 - 212
Drinking is a national sport
from San Francisco to Los Angeles to Chicago to New York

Sigmond
Gesturing Jester

On the subway from Wilshire to Hollywood, Siggy met
a lady* from Australia in a fashionable gray wool coat
*THIS could be "The One"
Subterranean Architectural Note –
   The Wilshire-Vermont subway station
   eastbound is 54 feet underground,
   westbound: 81 feet (simply count the steps)
May the skyscrapers here continue to scrape
 (and Not fall into the underground)

Hollywood Blvd at Las Palmas –
fresh-faced Salt Lake City debutante,
snazzy new black coat, brick-sized white purse
placed into her briefcase-sized black bag . . .

before long she & Sig were dancing right at the bar
she's showing him how to mirror her every move

putting ice cubes down his back and chest
and spanking him – so he returned the spank . . .
She says "No!" and spanks him even harder! . . .

She said, "I want to get laid tonight" but
apparently he's not at the Top of her pecking order.
Sig wishes her a safe night in her quest for love at 21

Side Note to Hanna Bartender –
  Sig can't say he's completely smitten
    but her aura is glowing

There are always warm people and cool times at
BJ's Burbank, Jamesons Hollywood, HMS Bounty Wilshire
and WIZNU Labs Studio on Spring Street

The writing life trumps the sex life –
That's why Sig will go for and input the keyboard
before going home with a creature on legs
(Sigmond sorting things out)

Journalist's Note –
  When you want to file your report after midnight
  but don't know if you can stay awake
  Take On a hot shower, blasting the spray into your face –
  No Sleep Until you Report!

"Spankin' Bottom" line –

You don't have to look elsewhere to be happy

Santa coming in for a landing . . . .

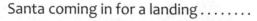

on ABC-TV: M-F nightly

time travelers 2105 & L.A. Red Line train station

Scene 4: As The Plot Thickens . . .

. . . and as the World Turns . . .

. . . That snazzy young lady from Salt Lake City
   is a showgirl at Hollywood & Vine Street *C'est la vie*!
   and THAT's just the tip of the ice nip

   Once again, back at the ranch (Fred 62)
   It looks like we won't have to wait until February
   for Princess Snowcastle – once you have seen the
   girl-next-door (and there's more than one door)

Feels Like Ascension
 When you are firing on all 8 cylinders of a
 4 cylinder engine, it's a rush that lifts you up . . .

like meeting new people

Phyllis Ophical Note:
 (priorities must prevail)
   How reality works (in our favor) –
   When something is not happening the way you expect,
   It is because other parts need to be developed first –
   and THEN the whole project can and will move forward
   and with better results. . . (add a few months in the process)

Loss prevention practice –
   As comfortable and secure as we may feel in a fast food / public place,
   we still need to hold onto our bag (of valuables, notes, etc.)
   to eliminate the temptation that we would otherwise provide

Smoothness of motion is the easier (harmonic) way
to go through life, especially when Driving –

 When your recreational level is up
 your driving rate of speed / showoff-ness should be lower

Photography Tip –
   when shooting a game of pool,
   shoot the break as a still or video
   for various visual impacts

Wordz of Wizdom --
   "The best way to get your heart going
   (besides aerobics) is sex with a pretty woman"
   according to Ray, former USC football champion

We Are One –
 make friends with everyone
   especially those on shaky ground
   who need your support

December Highlight –
Toy and canned food collection for Good Shepherd's
homeless women and children – at the clothing boutique
at 1616 Cahuenga in Hollywood, featuring acoustic and
electric guitar and vocals by Marissa Hollenback &
Chris Burkholder

Marissa VTR: Voice of Textured Resonance
her powerful vocals can make "water signs" cry
as her harmonic voice resonates
with the music collection of brain cells

Follow the bouncing ball at Johnny's Highland Park **&** CA Solar energy

Shibari Anya Knees & rigger Nikki at WIZNU Studio Labs **&** Northern California Sunset

Notable food (for thought) & Festive food at Fred 62

Scene 5: The CAT Is Out of the . . .

. . . yard It Fiddled in
so enchantingly, for so many years –
One life down, 8 to Go . . . .

(Cat & Fiddle garden pub closed 12/15/14, opened in 1984)
Moving Right Along . . .

Hanna and Rob will take nice care of you
at the rogue Rusty Mullet bar with its "social animals"
surrounded by more TV screens than the Dodgers have pennants
(and if the Dodgers feel a need for a little Penance –
perhaps the Angels can bestow forgiveness:
absolution absoLUTEly)

If you happen to find yourself in Burbank
amiable, respectable Rebecca (or Sophia)
will treat you right on Tuesday night

slide on over to BJ's bar-brewery-restaurant –

You can celebrate a bountiful Thanksgiving at
smile-inducing prices any Thursday at HMS Bounty on Wilshire
in the Old World elegance that is now Koreatown
Day bartender Noi knows your name And your *nom de plume*

On Friday, like Monday & Wednesday
Sig likes to attend (social studies) class at
Jamesons and the Rusty Mullet (bar next door)

Saturday afternoon, smart & cute actress Erin is likely
performing as the charming food service technician at the diner –

and at night there are "better to best" bands playing for a fun bunch of
folks at Scotland Yard on Sherman Way at Topanga Canyon Blvd

Sunday is the day to worship nature's majesty on

Mt. Wilson, Mt Lukens* (in La Crescenta) or Mt. Baldy locally
or Point Reyes (Marin County), Humboldt Redwoods State Park
or Mt. Shasta -- our northern neighbors . . . .

*on a Monday, there was a Holly blue-eyed blonde
moving – in two weeks with her group Y-WAM:
Youth With A Mission – to **Hawaii**. 'looks like she may
be "the One" even more than the One from Australia.
Also starting a new job in **Hawaii** is 'Remedy'
graduating from Northern Arizona

Babies for Jesus –
He: do you want to have children?
She: Yes, are you busy this afternoon?
He: I can Get Busy!

Monday-Sunday –
Jamesons, BJ's, Birds, HMS Bounty, Fred 62, Scotland Yard, mountains:
"That will Bring us Back to Doe: A Dear, A Female Dear /
Ray: a chap of bolden Fun …"

7 – A Versatile Number:
7 musical notes, 7 chakras, 7 colors, 7 days, 7 Sacraments

Here are the details:
  G: Crown, Violet, Sunday, Extreme Unction
  F: Third Eye, Indigo, Saturday, Holy Orders
  E: Throat, Blue, Friday, Matrimony
  D: Heart, Green, Thursday, Confirmation
  C: Solar, Yellow, Wednesday, Holy Communion
  B: Sacral, Orange, Tuesday, Penance
  A: Root, Red, Monday, Baptism

Happy Holidays, Christmas, Hanukkah
And Festivus* for the rest of us!

*a Seinfeld classic (1997)

Monday Night Highlight –
Unknowingly, Siggy's keys fell on the floor at Jamesons pub. As he
was walking out the front door, the man (resembling Michael Keaton)
sitting next to him alertly noticed them and rushed outside to hand him
the keys. Sig was SO grateful for this most fortunate event, he wanted
to give some dollars to someone ("pay it forward") as a reward for
being so well taken care of by a fellow person . . .

Sure enough, a man on Hollywood Boulevard made a brief & specific pitch
for $3 – so Sig gave him $3 and the man didn't ask for more (as they often do).

A moment later, another man told Sig his specific situation, asking for change or 5 or 10 dollars (emoting that the rain makes homelessness especially difficult). Sig replied that all he had left was change but the guy restated his serious need for 5 or 10 dollars. So Sig gave him a 5 – but he saw Sig's 10 and pleaded for that – so Sig said he'd give him the 10 in exchange for the 5 . . . He hesitated to give it back but sensed that he would have to, to get the 10. So they simultaneously exchanged bills – and Siggy was delighted!

Peace & Love (& Dollars)

Scene 1: A Soap Opera Is Born . . . (Dec 9)
Scene 2: (That's) Life In the Big City . . .
Scene 3: Multi-Lingual & Cunni-Lingual . . .
Scene 4: As the Plot Thickens . . .
Scene 5: The Cat Is Out of the . . .
Scene 6: From Sea Level To 7000 . . .

Scene 6: From Sea Level To 7000 . . .

Sea Level to the High, Pine country –

Los Angeles 57, Flagstaff 28 – Weather Permitting

~ A Feature Film ~
Starring
Michael Nemo and Signition 'Switch' Siggy
as NSA agents doing stand-up
When they're Not lying around . . .

or teaching young men
How & When to "Hold Their Horses"
(keeping "the boys" in the corral)

ID Question – Your Name or your Hometown area:
Which sounds more interesting?

Speaking of areas –
having reached heaven, Here is what That means:
sitting at a bar of 7 . . .

Upper Deck – Party of Seven:
Lisa Mademoiselle, Sarah* the playwright
Azida as Azalea Rhododendron Pentathera
Miss Texas as The Front Lady . . .
The cool & fun, Curiously Studious one who

photographs well in a Hudson River mansion +
Becky Rebecca & Sophia at a rival bar nearby

*Sarah: Look up the leading lady in TV's "The Avengers"
and see the elegant resemblance (Diana Rigg)

New careers for women – Bartenderess and Conductress
in the appropriate headdress

The more new people you meet
the more your life will be a treat

Back to the heaven reference – THIS is a place
to eat, drink and be merry
and ready for luck to embrace

What if people actually communicated This Way –
"You are 'superiorly' attractive
but I'm gonna go for the unattached writer"

In A Nutshell --
Food, frolic & whoopee: folks are always seeking it
'cuz That's how we were created/programmed/conditioned

Keeping It All Together –
The best way to misplace things is to
play musical chairs with all your pockets

Social Class: Upper to lower –
   Black Angus and Jack-In-The-Box
    are two & too opposite planets
     Two + Too = (~.~)

A Asian girl = "A" student + "A" personality

High (school) philosophy –
 Public school students should have pizza access daily
 "A" students may opt for Ahi too
 Personally, spinach with kryptonite
 is what makes Siggy rattle and hum

"On A Roll"
 (or jazzed by a caffeine muffin) . . . .

So, NOW we have to Write down EVERY Thing we Say?! –
    Oh, THIS is gonna be a royal pain-in-the-A!"

Speak with the tone that implies the right implication –
 Focused on your I.Q. (Intention Quest)

Sig's senior Friend in Hollywood is a funny yet acerbic reactor
and maybe a past life kingpin of the Medellin Cartel

Respect for elders – the 'remote' shall remain in their hand
       while they are still sentient . . . .

Semi-bottom line -- Confidence works when it offends no one
　　　　　　　　　(or is that "diplomacy")

Prop & Prognosis – Tuesday afternoon feelings:
The expertise of a woman is to know how to handle various scenarios
with strength of character, spirit of northern Kentucky charm
and height of glamor

What's This All About?
　　You know the future because you invent it
　　especially if it speeds up the human race
　　(not being the victim: but being the playwright!)

Bottom Line Mentality: mental immortality

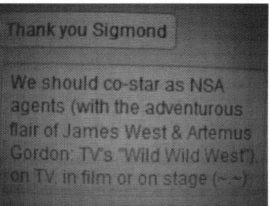

Thank you Sigmond

We should co-star as NSA agents (with the adventurous flair of James West & Artemus Gordon: TV's "Wild Wild West"), on TV, in film or on stage (~ ~)

Potato flower: radial six **&** accompanied by quesadilla

Burbank CA

$3 for each group: 3 to 6:30 PM & Blue C Sushi at Cinerama Dome

Scene 7: Ur Addiction's Siggy's Pleasure . . .

Cocky Hockey Productions Presents:

A Preeminent Nocturnal Telepathic transmission

Bonus Feeling –
   Ya Don't need to go to Malibu to feel sunny-**warm** & peach-**fuzzy** –
   Ye Rustic Inn will do THAT for You In a Minute!

To Bartenderess Allie J –
   "This beer is Just the Right Temperature
   And Just the Right Flavor"
   Crisp Liquid Bread
   The King of Beers

Karen at the Inn –
   Her graceful aura is a kindred
   spiritual twin of Princess Snowcastle:
   both having the Helen Hunt essence/effervescence

Bar Wisdom – "At Least Sig Knows Something!"
   Sauza Tequila – like Cutty Sark Scotch –
   Goes down Real Easy (like a smooth gal)

A Perfect Game (going all 9 Innings)
   Is Pacing yourself through 9 servings of beer
   while maintaining a perfect pitch

The Speed of the Read –

   If you can't Keep Up with this Breathtaking Pace*
   Take a Breath Mint

* 2 new scenes coming out every 4 days . . . .
   but at This point: Twice a day (12 hour cycle)

Sex does not require excessive self-indulgence
   like a big plate of chili cheese fries with Wings

Accidentally Doing the Right Thing –
   When you can't find something when out & about
   it may be because You had Already Thought it Better
   To leave it (a non-essential) at home ...
   So, You Didn't Lose It After All! Yeah!

California Bar Guide --
   Mt. Shasta -- Wayside Inn; Gold Room
   Eureka – The Shanty; Speakeasy
   Redway – Brass Rail
   Shelter Cove – Mario's
   Occidental – Negri's / Union Hotel . . .
   San Francisco -- Night Cap; Noc Noc
   San Luis Obispo – Buffalo Pub & Grill
   Santa Barbara – Sand Bar
   Ojai -- Deer Lodge; Ojai Beverage Co.
   Channel Islands – Whale's Tail; Rudder Room
   Ventura – Sans Souci; The Tavern
   Malibu – Duke's; Neptune's Net
   Venice -- O'Brien's Oar House

Santa Monica – Ye Old King's Head
Canoga Park – Scotland Yard / Casey's
Tujunga – Crows Nest Sports Bar
Burbank – BJ's / Black Angus
Glendale – Golden Road Brewery / Big Fish Bar
Studio-Universal City – The Fox and Hounds / Univ Bar & Grill
Hollywood – Jamesons / Rusty Mullet
Hollywood outskirts – Birds on Franklin
Los Feliz – Ye Rustic Inn* Drawing Room
Wilshire – HMS Bounty
Downtown – Bar 107; Edison
Pasadena – 35er; Old Towne Pub
Mt. Wilson -- Newcomb's Ranch
Mt. Baldy -- Top of The Notch
West Covina – Lucille's Barbeque
Redlands -- Barnacles; Hangar 24

Today's New Anagram –

prosperous ET = preposterous
   {THAT Is just Too Cool!}
For more of these mind ticklers:
consult *Twayne's Mental Cookbook*
       (authorhouse.com)

Sincerely and Rocketometricly,

Wernher von Bunsen-Burner
with Svetlana Swizzleschein:
Siggy's lab partners

---

* try a "New Fangled" by Lexistential Designs Studio

Does a polar bear sit on the Holiday Inn lawn?

square meal: Tacos to Live For!

see Scene 1 & Griffith Observatory, L.A

Scene 8: Ascend With The Reindeer !!!!

Art of Socialization –
  Expectable Waiting Time:
    (pay your dues in minutes)
When you arrive in a bustling place
and there's barely a seat to sit on,
you have to wait a bit
until your opening move (2A seat at the bar)
manifests in a warmly interactive way –
When your number is called, figuratively,
You shall be Up and Ready to go
~ ~ ~ ~ ~ ~ ~ ~ ~ ~ ~ ~ ~ ~ ~ ~ ~ ~ ~

When You're In the Area --
  Barstow – hooz on first (Maria)
  Weed – Papa's Place (Raechel), Mt. Shasta Brewing
  Weaverville – Diggins Bar
    (between Mt. Shasta & Humboldt Forest)

Writers/Actors Note -- If you create a monster
        you better be strong enough to wrestle with it
                        until it matures

Fine tune your writing as you fine tune your audience
of reciprocal recipients (readers <-> respondents)

Anti-Aging Dream – Have you ever been over the hill, wanting
      to use those magical new-age soaps –
      just to wash the years off your face?

Concept of engagement – functionality of a year-long engagement
      is to prove that there's no other person
      who can supersede the chosen one Or
      to have a few flings until the time comes
      to settle up with the life partner . . .
      You can meet the perfect woman:
      you'll find there are hundreds of them
      from Vermont Avenue to Vermont State

Rising Star Audrey – She has a certain sense of brightness
      at planet 9: screen-tested, audience-approved
      & her BIC Round Stic is now a celebrity souvenir

Hanna Bartenderess – She is pretty perfect looking –
      does that ever start to bother her?
      In other words, she's elegantly glamorous:
      Is she always comfortable with that? . . .
      "What One thing might she not like about herself?"

Erin: Sig gave it some serious thought
  and decided to adopt her
  but now he's mellowed out
  and feeling more independent

Ma Jo Ro: Sig loves every inch of every stitch of fine fabric on her

Source code:
    Courteney   ~.~
    Sophia   {~.~}
    Chloe   ({~.~})
    Erin   (~.~)
    Maggie Jo   XOXO

~ ~ ~ ~ ~ ~ ~ ~ ~ ~ ~

Just Being Human – learn to control your emissions
                whether as a writer / speaker
                or just a water passer (a conduit)
                Be the special breed that can hold their own

Path to Ascension -- Helping your fellow creatures:
                You don't have to get All Righteous
                 if a bug walks into your house:
                They are living souls – and like us
                some are looking forward to a better life.
                So, just say to him or her
                "You're going to heaven" in a supportive,
                assuring, uplifting tone – as you send the
                little pioneers on their way (out of their
                bodies with a quick, decisive contact)

~ ~ ~ ~ ~ ~ ~ ~ ~ ~ ~ ~ ~ ~ ~ ~ ~ ~ ~ ~

Silent Music, Holy Music
  by Brain Spritzer instruments "Stray CAT-scan Thrust"

Here's a song about another cool cat . . .

(e-Book link: Beach Boys "Little Saint Nick")

http://tinyurl.com/nzuax7m

Bride Zilla custom designs Hollywood Blvd & lily
dancer in white pointing to upper right

Holiday Greetings from the monk

Scene 9: Board the Mothership . . .

. . . It takes just a few minutes to board the Mothership:

http://tinyurl.com/qdrp8cv

Immoral or Immortal – THAT Is the Question!

What everybody thinks (when in tune),
"I wanna rock you until your eyes expand
  like the gleaming blue marble universe"
  Or "until they glow like extraterrestrial orbs"
  -- Cosmic Love Guide

Industrial Strength Pick-up Line –
"I'm gonna make your nips stand up & shoot out sparks!"

You can tell when an awkward couple is on a date:
not knowing who they are or what they want . . .

Men's common Mis Perception –
  Although "getting lucky" is all it's cracked up to be
  It's NOT the total appreciation/approval they are seeking

If your love is so perfect, you need to have a baby
so the 2 of you can enjoy together checking its diapers
after just doing the wild thing

Children: The Dilemma – YOU created them
                         So What'd you Expect!
                         Carl Sagan?

Reproduction -- What is the Point of having children . . .
                         Unless they can trump themselves above
                         the rest of the flock, herd, talking heads?

Here Is the Career -- Notice and develop all the fluent talents
                         and get them the residuals they deserve
                         (after they star in the commercials)

"Casper" The Friendly Blonde Pale Ale
                play so smoothly by an actress up on Vine –
                moving up the movie ladder, she'll see some fans
                weak-in-the-knees ('cuz she IS drop-dead gorgeous)
                as they adjust to their first time watching her
                on the silver screen

Stars and their fellow planets rule the cosmos
"lock, cockstock & barrel" – on the jumbotron

Driving Half the world Crazy
& the Other half doesn't know King Jack yet

Sigmond
Ahi Tuna King
& Jack of Salmon

At home . . . & . . . with Santa

a colorful life **&** pair of pairs, 6751 Hollywood Blvd

Early & late model Firebirds **&** pair of 'birds en route to Jamesons

Scene 10: -> Lucid Acid {~.~} . . .

. . . The Hits Just KEEP ON COMING!

This list of "Most Intense Aromas"
Just "Caught Fire" on Saturday night:
  Here's What We Have So Far . . . .

Roses
lemon
honey
Shalimar Passion White Diamonds

White Shoulders:

Top Notes
Neroli, Tuberose, Aldehydes

Middle Notes
Gardenia, Jasmine, Orris, Lily of the Valley, Rose, Lilac
Base Notes
Sandalwood, Amber, Musk, Oakmoss

pine
coffee
eucalyptus
menthol (Vicks)
sage incense
BACON french fries
hot creosote (railroad tie tar)

patchouli oil
crispy hot wings (scorched vinegar)
liquid p (musky fresh)
sulphur (hot springs)
~ ~ ~ ~ ~ ~ ~ ~ ~ ~ ~ ~ ~ ~ ~ ~
// /// //// ///// \\\\\ \\\\ \\\ \\

A Plethora of Sarahs nowadays –

  Sarah (visiting with friend M at Jamesons)

    Sarah Screenwriter at a steakhouse

      Sarah editor at a weekly newspaper

      and I guess Hanna(h) is Not Sara(h)

     but Sarah Jean is an ace to the queen

    as co-founder of new band "The Shitwhippers"

with the Sigmonster . . . . .

O.K: THAT's the Warm Up –
Here's the skinny. The scoop. The dish.

"Board The Mothership"

  Courtney, Josh, Ryan, Audrey

  with Hanna Savannah Sarah Jean

  Erin Sophia "Miss W Texas" Luke Aaron

  The Dashing Dozen

The Mothership's high-pitch electric guitar
  will tickle your pineal gland . . .

Now teleport to the scene

at Auto Club Speedway ->

with Aaron/Speed Ventures
    Courtney in the front passenger seat
    Drummer & bassist in the back seat:
    Chevy SS 140 "Cobalt Muthaship"

Hypothetical *amore* pro bono cameo
by Eminem & Rihanna (a grand duet)

and one number by Junction Lawn

http://tinyurl.com/kv7tpo6

~ ~

Tom	Sig
1983 The Outsiders	20XX Board The Mothership (producer)
1983 Risky Business	20XY Lucid Acid
1985 Top Gun	20XZ Night of The Ascension
~ ~ ~ ~ ~ ~ ~	~ ~ ~ ~ ~ ~ ~
Nicole	Taylor S'Barbara

Regarding Kellie Ann –
Usually men don't like being with a woman shopping –

But in HER case, Sig is There! All The Way! And THEN Some …
  When he met Her, he struck gold (she's 50: her face looks 25!)
  She is the petite glowing angel at the top of the holiday tree.
Sweet princess of neverland:
  She claims to be 50 – Sig Claims Her for Spain!
  That's his Christopher Columbus jubilation

Farm Talk –
  squeezing the trickle out of a peter hose
  can be like milking an udder

Thoughts on the Move –
  Once you have a thought, it cannot be destroyed
  although it may have floated away
  See: *Twayne's Mental Cookbook*, p. 605

History –
  Ben Franklin would've given his right nut for a day surfing the net

Infatuation –
  Ms. Sarah Jean: Connecti-cute!
  Save your organic energy for the morning.
  WHY are she and Sig so 'perfect' together and
  why does he have the habit of feeling this way ? ?

  Can you IMAGINE what four hands feeling
  the petite golden gem is going to Be Like!

Thrill ride –
   The man locked onto a target of solid movie vehicles
   Then Sci-optology hijacked his sky-high trajectory
   Sig loves him and his dynamic cinematic art

Sigmond Snot* the Snooty One
                    *is not

And Finally –
   Creating deep bonds
   based on common goals/activities –

   As Shakespeare might say
   "It's Time to Do your Thing"
   And Sarah Jean is in the ring!

nachos drenched

Burbank CA

Scene 11: ~~ Tea Leaves & Legible Pants ~~

Emily & Becca Present:
old-fashioned not-so-square style
at the classic rustic Scotland Yard: (e-Book link)

http://tinyurl.com/qdumet8

Places To Go – In the post-Christmas Spirit
Crows Nest -- Tujunga Ray

Scotland Yard* -- Canoga Park Becca Emily

Paolis karaoke -- Woodland Hills: Sundays

BJ's Black Angus – The Party of Seven

UB&G*** -- Sarah Jean, Kellie Ann, Art of Emmanuel

Jamesons Rusty Mullet – Aaron Alexandra Luke Hanna, Rob

9 O V – Audrey Savannah

HMS Bounty – Noi, John Juan, Suzanne & the gang

Sigmond
"Busier than a 1-legged man in a soccer game"
   (or a butt-kicking contest, if you prefer)

*** ZEISTENCROIX dazzles at **U**niversal **B**ar & **G**rill

http://tinyurl.com/qcc5r4o

*Tea Leaves – some people read them –
   but Sig reads women's legs (pants) . . .
   the first one read "LAWRENCE" (letters: top to bottom)
   (And Her Name is **Jennifer**)

A Mantra Is Born --On the fifth day before Christmas, Sig began
                     his new mantra-esque phrase "I love you"
                     which means "You're a wonderful person"

Jump In Now -- support the mentally handicapped
                     but don't Do It with them
                     (After that first spirited acrobatic fling)
                     Not just a hot mess – a unique eccentric

Common human flaw -- when a person is not getting satisfaction
                     from being busy Doing things –
                     They try getting it From Buying things!

Worse Yet – thieves are woefully unaware of karma
               (if not driven by desperation of starvation)

The Haves & the Have-Nots –
   People who work for a living make the extra effort to be nice
   to their customers and other people. Some corporate globalists
   who have Never needed money to survive, make the extra effort
   to cause ordinary people to be uncomfortable, sick or dead to
   make massive profits. That's the current state of the world
   But THAT Is Going to Change!

Corrupt Corporatist's most realistic Fear –
   Reincarnating as a career homeless person:
   a Life Sentence of poverty and humility,
   living WITHOUT a shopping cart on the street
   rather than in a mansion with a fleet of jets . . .
   Join the Club! of Homelessness – which they
   helped create with their "trickle down" economics
   (as in "pee on the peons")

Flawless --   the 3-story condo being built next door
Construction   has a steel 'I'-beam "floor bone" (see photo: p. 50)
                  along the middle of the base of the 3rd floor
"Ain't No earthquake gonna Shake THAT mutha down!"

         "It Ain't Over Until . . . The Fat wallet Sings" –
   The entire military-medical-insurance-bankster structure
         could "collapse" once Lucky 7 Larry says "Pull It"
         (when they're That far above the law – the bigger the
         scam, the higher the federal promotion: muck easy)

Last And Surely Least -- V.C. Viet Cong Ventura County (see photo: p. 50)
                  Don Ho IS A Ho – but he was born That way!

Sigmond
THE COMPLETE COOKIE

Hot bands and cool people

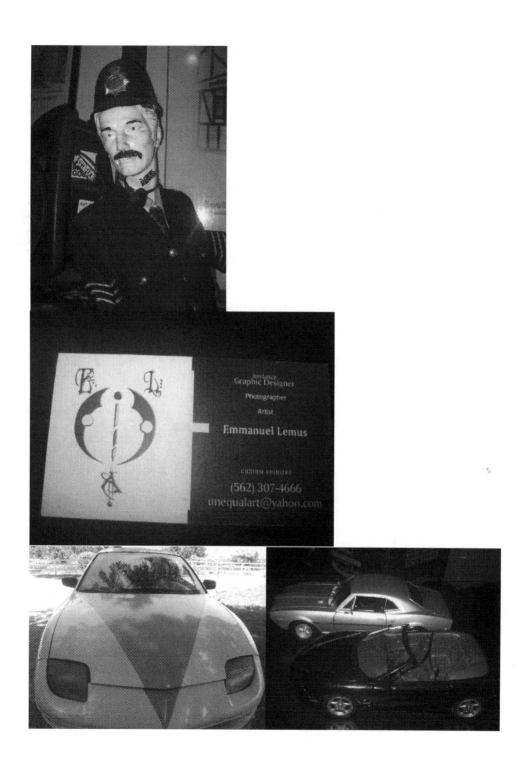

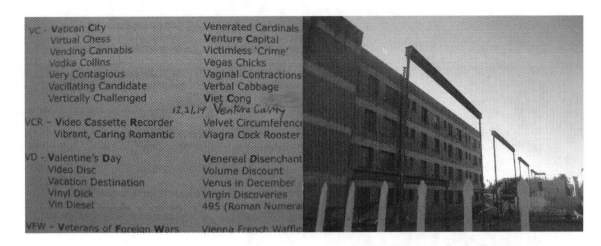

All Things VC, VCR & VD (page 334 of Twayne's Mental Cookbook) &
Earthquake-resistant steel 'backbone' to hold up the 3rd floor

Scene 12: "2670 Reindeer Terrace" . . .

. . . Monday Solstice Madness!

Some Bel-Air solstice parties are like an
exercising, living cemetery (of cemeterians)

It's on a Tributary in Purgatory
~ ~ ~ ~ ~ ~ ~ ~ ~ ~ ~ ~ ~ ~ ~ ~ ~

. . . meanwhile, across the stream (of Mercedes-Benzedream)
"Santa, You've got (how many?:) 6, 8, 10, 12 perfect reindeer here:
More red Scotch plaid skirts than you can shake a candy cane at!"
A pretty nice preview of heaven

Necessary & Sufficient –
It is necessary that you be a looker
but that is not sufficient – We'd like
a colorful brain in fine working order:
"a smooth blend of Warhol Woody Allen
Joe Walsh and Neil Young artistry"

Sig Doesn't even Wear pants anymore –
just black tights – Zorro Is Back!
with a XX Dos Equis six-pack

Au Contraire! -- maybe you don't know this
       and Sig barely does Himself: He's in a boy band
       with Sam & the other two – they are Salsa Picante
       (sponsored by United Colors of Benevolence)

Also developed at solstice party –
   "Country Grunge" – The folks just coined a new genre
     for *Billboard* to get all drooly about – & bait them
       with the debut album "Home On the Road"

The Lesson Sig has learned is to be less about him & more about you –
That may be How he gathers more moss than a rolling stone . . . . .

What's Happening – Sig's mind straight into your e-mail inbox:
                    feed your inbox some nutrients (with music)

Quadrophonic :: Glenn Miller Tommy Dorsey
                    Artie Shaw Harry James

Listening & Dancing, Eating & Drinking –
            choose the Wild West Onion Rings
                    OR the mildly docile onion wannabes . . .

http://tinyurl.com/lctcosg

            If you've been sitting still for awhile
            and you drink 4 pints of beer (in 2 hours)
            you may feel like you're 4 months pregnant
            and That's stretchin' the ol' tummy

Round Notes for an All-Around Girl—
(drink coaster notes)
1. Sig wants to run a tab with you – all the way –
   to Las Vegas
2. He trusts your brain
3. Do you concentrate better after you inhale?
4. He is so ready to jump in a car with you but shall defer until tomorrow

Word progression – Silver - Gold - Platinum - Titanium
        Humongous - Ginormous - Colossal - Stupendous

Basketball Games – are kind of fun: watching those long lanky trees
                falling all over each other like collapsible Gumbies

Speaking of Male Prowess – Possible & Probable:
                2B in luv with 2 women concurrently
                but Will they blend together in harmony?
                Ask Wilt The Stilt

Christmas Valentine to Sig's role model –
to develop the best relationships
until it's time to settle up with MJR

All Sig wants from Santa: "Presents of Mind"
(if the jolly old one has any left)

Exit Line – "When the Sun comes up tomorrow, think of me . . .
  Make some coffee and put me in as the cinnamon"

Sigmond American cinnabon
and card-carrying member of the SS
or maybe the NSA (No Such Agency)
or NASA (Never A Straight Answer)

Scene 13: Special Ed. . . .

Not originally intended as Scene 13
But as a special edition –
An "aside" (if not a soliloquy) –
for any Spear shaker or billiard ballplayer
of either gender . . . .

see photo on next page

"RACK 'EM UP!"

Nose of the Eightball -
1. MJRPNW
2. SJUB&G
3. KAUB&G
4. Aud9V
5. HannRM
6. SophiBJS
7. RebecBJS
8. EriF62
9. Savan9V
10. KatiePNW
11. Alona1739PH
12. JessiF62
13. SLCgirl
14. DaeshaInn
15. AnyRustican (e-Book link: billiards & other videos)

http://tinyurl.com/q7woa65

What is so special about *MJR?!* –
　　Tall blonde from So. Illinois-Kentucky (SILKY)
　　with a casual Charm & Glow, who will
　　Take Hollywood by Storm –
　　If not by Comet!

Writers' Note –
　　Think retrospectively
　　It helps clear the mind

P.S. It's nice when a young lady
　　walks with you more than a half mile to
　　Bronson on Sunset from Fountain & Vine
　　where the party started

Crows Nest Sports Bar, Tujunga CA

Scene 14: HOT OFF The PRESS!..

Ever Been On a Superdate?...

Go to Cho-Sun Korean barbeque on Olympic

Then ride to Las Vegas
    from Hollywood with Sosh of Norway

This is a premature valentine to one Violet of the spectrum –

American Woman – L.A. Woman – Oh Yeah!
This woman is funnier, smarter & prettier than f'n Anyone!

Cleopatra Elizabeth
~~ Kape Taylor of L.A. ~~

The car goes 135 in the desert on the way to Vegas
Let's Git 'er DONE! Tonight – "You're Ready to Go!"
It Will Be Filmed
Cool as that may seem
Some will become recognized "stars"
and wardrobe will Treat you Well –

Lady Violette has the eye vision of a hawk
with tuned radar and savvy intuition

The Happiest Place On Earth Is Not What You've Been Told!
But Rather It Is 5153 Hollywood Boulevard, Of Course!
Angel Face Spirit of Chelsea, Oh So Fine Lux & soul twin Gemini
Cherry On Top looks better than ever (to everybody's delight)

Let's Cover this –
    Mayan Calendar: Dec 2012 of course was Not the end
    But a new cycle now firing on all 12 cylinders of the zodiac!

When It's Time to Ascend – You Will Know!

The lovely ETaylor-Violette is a young Veronica Lake

Violette: This One's for You . . . . (Sweetest Taboo)

http://tinyurl.com/o79mbkd

Violette: and This One's for You Too . . . . (Bad Girls)

http://tinyurl.com/pywv5rh

Feel The Love –

Scene 15: Koalabear Lumpur . . .

Dubai Or Not Dubai
To Spend* or Not to spend
*buy gold when u have the cash

~ Immoral or Immortal ~
Decadence or Ascension (or Both!)
\|/ Wrestle with the motion of That notion /|\

U.A.E. That's where our girl Chloe Chloacious Is!

>   She is living the life that the untraveled
>   Western Hemispherians can only imagine
>   ~

"California" -- Montalvo's imaginary island paradise:

There's a mythical island called "California"
ruled by Queen Calafia and warrior women "of vigorous
bodies and strong and ardent hearts and of great strength."
The queen and her warriors venture forth on forays,
where they seize and kill men they come upon.
Any man found in their domain, they eat.

Although sometimes they have children from those they
make peace with, they keep only daughters and murder sons.
It is a land near the Terrestrial Paradise, where the only metal in
existence is gold. A land where griffons abound, which the women take
as pets and feed to them the men they capture and the sons they bear.

Where Montalvo got the idea for the name 'California' remains unknown
but several plausible theories exist. One idea holds that it stems from an
Islamic term for leader: "caliph." The Spanish equivalent being "Calif."

In Montalvo's novel, Queen Calafia is a sovereign ruler
who is allied with infidels against Muslims. Thus the name
"California" is a logical designation for the land she ruled

"Sounds Like" – This parking lot is pretty full – that's Pitiful!
　　　　　　　But That lot is ALL Full – that's Awful!! . . .
　　　　　　　meanwhile, 'didn't mean to be mean to Armenia
　　　　　　　but will still be an attorney for eternity where it's
　　　　　　　usually one case of perjury per jury in purgatory
　　　　　　　while Venice's wailin' for Venezuela!
　　　　　　　(and You & I scream for Ice Cream)

Life in Unitopia – The 51st State
Bill of Rights (those that are still left)

1. Herbal coffee
2. Nozzle shots (hot shower)
3. YouTube
4. the Red tube:
5. Red Line * to Universal City
6. Mental Cookbook readings
7. More clarity of perception
8. 5153 Hollywood musical gymnasts
9. Point & shoot (pen & camera)
10. Precision driving

* http://tinyurl.com/naac4g3

Riddle –

#1,2,3 are silver, #4 dark red, #5 black. What Am I?

[Canon PowerShot: 2004-2014]

Construction is BOOMING in L.A. **&** Sunset & Vine

Blue C Sushi

Lists at $399 & sells for $249

Scene 16: Fresh Starts START Daily . . .

How To Craft A Draft --
The newest torch (latest flame) is at Islands . . .

HELLO! My Name Is . . .
[*in stylized handwriting*]
   Sampan Pita
   Sampan Playa
   Samantha
     scientist - hostess - ballet dancer

Her Bottom line: she's got the roundest rear for a slim one
             with not an ounce of fat – but pounds of brains sterling

"Virginia is for Lovers" -- but California is for hotter buns

Bartenderesses have always been a favorite species (class of people) . . .
       . . . NOW They are evolved Star Vehicles
         ~

Look Over There! – at the end of the bar:
        a lady is driving her lips into his –
        does that imply he'll be driving his pile driver
        into the pliable bedrock tonight?

Shift Into Glide –
    A person feeling jealous
    halfway across the planet
    can cause a hiccup in the Earth's rotation
    (and in her lover's outward momentum)

'jealousy' – a feeling arising from a needy,
                false sense of ownership / control
                (we've all been thru it)

About to affiliate with an unnumbered
number of starlets and other artists:
thus wanting to "plant the tent pegs"
with Ma Jo Ro sooner than later
(re: Mystic Hot Springs Utah February)

Sig may as well Be Committed!
~ ~ ~ ~ ~ ~ ~ ~ ~ ~ ~ ~ ~ ~ ~ ~ ~

Afterthought -- The human brain has a LOT of pores to be filled –
                Visit your local mixologist

Pharmacological Philosophy –
    Never do more mind-sharpening herbs than you can handle –
    Nor Less!

Why? – Curiosity (may have) killed the cat
  but it made scientists glow late into the night

Damon's Steakhouse & Glendale CA

Scene 17: Bet On Car #24 – Lifestyle by Sophia

In your extended social life, if you ever get mixed up
about who's who – it's because there are several people
playing the same character . . .

Birth of a Camera Presents:

Twins of Other Families

	1st Set		2nd Set	
	Heather	Rebecca	Sophia	Gabrielle
	/\	/\	/\	/\
	Dennys	BJ's	BJ's	Lucille's BBQ

Sophia & Rebecca – One Hot Item
      at one wonderful restaurant!

Sophia makes the future seem So much better
mainly because Sig just purchased a share of it
[he has the receipt]

She seems too usefully efficient & practical
to play a vamp or chanteuse #24
but Sig's been wrong before

On the last day of the year
there are more galz buzzing around
than stars have planets

'looks like the Burbank brunette psych grad
is on par with all princesses who make us glad –

Sophia, Samantha, Rebecca –
    S, S, R & Sig together could very well herald
    the beginning of a new energy civilization

Dreams = Twisted Theatre of the subConscious
                Ask ANYONE Who's Been There!

Having found our human equilibrium
Now we can all feel the love:
    all crimes come to an end
     all debts are cancelled
      all bankers are mortified
        all billionaires are stunned
          all truthful writers are welcomed
~ ~ ~ ~ ~ ~ ~ ~ ~ ~ ~ ~ ~ ~ ~ ~ ~ ~ ~

Fill your tank on 8 craft drafts
& you'll be 1 step above 7th heaven

Catholichurch familiar? –
   Sig was a parochial inpatient for 8 years
   in Bergen County New Jersey
   in Wyckoff NJ –
   "Why cough when you can sneeze?" (the town joke)

Let's Go Deeper –
   Men & women – **m**utt **b**ostly* Dogs *(a spoonerism)
   know Not to get too close
   'cuz Sig's mind might bite 'em from 6 feet away

Final Sermon – Sig Doesn't Wanna Die:
   NOT Because he's afraid –
   but because he doesn't want to See EVERYTHING at Once!
   You see, right here & right now in this: the 3rd density
   there's Already So much Overlapping . . .

   BJ's Brewhouse, 1899 Bar & Grill (Northern Arizona Universe)
   Lucille's BBQ, Islands, 9 On Vine, Universal Bar & Grill

   mahi mahi at Islands -- mahi mahi at BJ's

   The World Is Getting In Synch: The place for everyone to think

Hugh Mility
Sig's Life Coach

Bonus Video – Red Line on the Fast Track
               Arriving at Universal City (e-Book link)

http://tinyurl.com/morgymu

UFO (Unidentified Found Object) & BJ's Brewhouse (in 19 states)

Scene 18: Deja Vu: harmoniConvergence . . .

. . . All OVER Again! . . .

as we all gracefully glided across the December-January line –
We are now Feeling and exhibiting our exhilarating *savoir faire*
{artistic skills} among one another with fluency and frequency

And THAT's HOT! – Thank You to the entire MIX 96.9 staff:

Adam Alexandra Amanda Amber Amy
Cassie Chelsea Chloe Daesha Deb Deja Delilah
Eliza Emmie Erin Fiona Gaby Gemini Hanna
Heather Holly Isabel Jaime Jil Kari Katie Kellie-Ann
Kendra Kristyn Lenore Lindsey Madeline Mallory Meredy
Mindy Moriah Nataly Raechel Rebecca Sage Samantha
Sarah-Jean Sarah-Screenwriter Savannah Shelby Simone
Sophia Stefanie Taylor Topaz Whitney Zack

How does One keep Track of all this?

With One's 3rd Eye (& a pen)

Musical example. . . . . . . (e-Book link: Beach Boys "I Get Around"

http://tinyurl.com/jqnfffc

We've Come a Long Way
To be among the emerging leaders:

The Future Is Ours to Have and to hold
where people don't get tired or old

With Love & Hugs,

Liquid Lucy {~.~}
Siggy's spirit guide

the moon as a) Tennis ball . . . & . . . b) baseball . . .

. . . c) soccer ball **&** 1927 Tudor, architect E.P. Chapman

photo: c Gabriel Milori, Brooks Institute of Visual Arts, Ventura CA
brooks.edu **&** anti-particle beam towers

Scene 19: NOT The Same Person . . .

. . . that Sigmond was in the 20th century . . .

This is the current person –

To push back a cold from taking hold:
Sig drinks water with Ester-C powder
tastes like dirt

To push back cancer to oblivion
eat apricot kernels
taste like flavored dirt

& because coffee is generally healthful
drink Folgers classic roast
tastes not at all like dirt

As another health booster
eat a full mouthful of broccoli sprouts
tastes like broccoli with a zesty kick

garlic, onion, cucumber, watercress,
spinach, romaine, tomato, avocado,
sauerkraut, tempeh, yogurt,
dark chocolate & red wine top off
the way never to get sick-ill-
under-the-weather again . . .

Now Fasten Your Eyeglass-belts –

We're About To Get Started:
shoot your arrows straight $\rightarrow$

Sigmond
Actor Comic DJ
Photo-videographer Video 57 reviewer
Traveling health adviser YouTube Channeler

New England August **&** Chevy Cobalt SS

Ben thinks for a moment **&** "She's Got Legs!" at Glendale Galleria

Scene 20: 2 Photos & 1 Steamy Video

Going All The Way on the First Day –
  Isn't THAT the Most Natural?
~ ~ ~ ~ ~ ~ ~ ~ ~ ~ ~ ~ ~ ~ ~ ~

   D-Kay says

her vibration alone moves people's
consciousness into the Center of their hearts
so their minds start to Purify more

   Sigmond says

his vibration alone makes most dogs bark
in a rage of perplexed trepidation
   (his expansive Thoughtsphere
      prob'ly gives them a headache)
~ ~ ~ ~ ~ ~ ~ ~ ~ ~ ~ ~ ~ ~ ~ ~ ~

D-Kay: Sig might say
U R Turning him On
in a spiritual kinda Way

Sig's new Consciousness makes him a very suggestive being –
   He suggests dinner at Cho-Sun Korean barbeque
      and then *après ski* (after party) at home

Hillary Newcomer –
   Sig likes your look of perky thoughtfulness

/The satellite Way Up over your head is looking toward your future\

Real Estate Mantra – "Location, Location, Location"
      Artistic Mantra – "Process, Process, Process"

Steamy Video – http://tinyurl.com/q6bgs3k

Illuminati Note –
   Humans are the highest form of programmable sheep (sheeple)

Hope – Future & Present:
   Don't let your dramatic / traumatic past
   Keep you Now from going from slow to Fast

Divine Providence –
   Even if Greg Garious could score TODAY
   it may Not be his best move

Critics Rave! – "Sigmond is like Woody Allen on Acid!"
               (a matter of spectacular speculation)

As drops of beer playfully precipitate on Sig's writing paper . . .

The MIX 96.9 member pod
has grown into this "Top 60" –
Alicia Alexandra Amanda Amber Audrey Ava
Cassie Chelsea Chloe Daesha Deb Deja Dena Delilah Devai
Eliza Emmie Erin Fiona Gaby Gemini Hanna Heather
Hillary Holly Isabel Jacqui Jaime Jil Kari Katie Kellie-Ann
Kendra Kristyn Lenore Lux Madeline Maggie-Jo Mallory Meredy
Mindy Moriah Nataly Patience Raechel Rebecca Sage Samantha
Sarah-Jean Sarah-Screenwriter Savannah Shelby Simone
Sophia Stefanie Taylor Topaz Whitney Ziggy Zoe

~.~.~.~.~.~

Spirited Bottom Line:

We ARE a protected species:
LOOK at how Much we've done for one another!
--))---)))----))))----)))))------))))))-------)))))))--------))))))))---------)))))))))----------))))))))))

COMING SOON:
    "Better Than Paris -> A Savvy Look at the New American Woman"

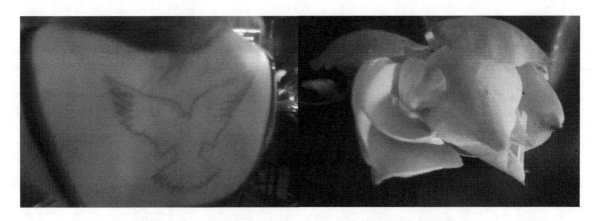

Hillary displays her art & . . . like a gorgeous gladiola

Scene 21: Self-Indulgence as an Art Form . . .

Incidentally,
　do you ever get emotionally exhausted?

It HAPPENS – like about every two or three months!

OK, 'Got THAT Out of the Way!

Now Let's Indulge –

　A Quick Shout-Out to Sig's virtual valentine of the future:

He Knows this is not Valentine's Day
　　Nor is it Valentine's Month!

So he 'must' be out-of-synch:
Is he wrong to have chemistry (instinctive attraction)
with the starlet from the North end of the South? ...
　Where Illinois & Kentucky get their groove on
　　in a harmoniously circuitous border dance . . .

She has a down-home saintliness
(with the light charm) that will always
make him feel like he's met the right people

Others may come closer in psychological complementalism
(complementarianism / compatibility) or social acceptability –
  but he's trying to decode and adhere to the path that was
    supposedly planned during the "between lives" cycle . . . .

Until his head is out of the clouds, he shall
  wear his heart on an Ascension Gown

For the people of Earth –
  The First Monday of the Year
    Shall henceforth be celebrated as
      "Declaration of Self-Indulgence" Day

Now, ON With the SHOW!

(e-Book link: peacock sound) http://tinyurl.com/am43nub

peacock photo: Ana Isabel Arbogast, Puerto Vallarta, Mexico, June 2014

Scene 22: No One Said "Heaven . . .

. . . Is Going To Be Easy ...

Especially The 1st Week:

  an eMotional rOllErCOAsTeR

(Magic Mountain will help you prep)

Upon arriving on "Avenue of The Angels"
You'll have to get a grip on Your feelings for
the panoramic procession of perfect beings

All THAT And a travel date too: February– to God's grotto

Mystic Hot Springs Utah -- paradise on earth
                    And in Steamy Hot Pools!

Shall We Move On . . . Let's PLAY a little .....

B:) Brenna Rhea: Role Model & *Shibari* artist-performer
    and best inspiration for the talented to BE Their best
c): cel phones: remedial social devices
D:) Deja: view a virtual harmoniConvergence
e): expediency: keep your love letters in proper order
f:) future: as U see the future coming in, wrangle It
g:) gateway: there's a portal to paradise-heaven
    at El Matador beach on P.C.H.

h:) hot: when U are Hot (ON your Game, IN your Zone)
you can deliver a few lines & write some sizzling new ones

a:) amorous: Ms. Bartenderess, do you mind if Sigmonster
eats while YOU are still hungry?

RS – Rally Sport:

R & S – At The Bar!

If Yer a-Hankerin' fer some fun:
Come to **BJ's*** around 6 to 9
 (No private invitations will be issued)

* http://www.bjsrestaurants.com

Siggy's Subscribers Note –

This scene is #22 of a series
For the titles of any or all 22, send a self-addressed e-velope to us

And **Huell** & I will "Get it Out to You RIGHT AWAY!"

Fred 62 serves the finest outlaws

West Coast Distributing, Tujunga CA & 'steam punk' at Birds

Scene 23: Ye Happiest Place On Earth

BJ's is a succulent name for a bar-rewery

And the bartenderesses are highly engageable –
Rebecca is a fine example
Sophia could be Sig's psych advisor . . .

Oh Well, Tuesday shall live on Forever
~ ~
Flashing back to Saturday

-- To Ye Happiest Place on Earth –
Tattoos are starting to grow on Siggy
Thanks to KIM – Our Lady of Class & Spunk
~.~ (luv manifests in many ways) ~.~

If you serve Sig enough beers
-- and detain him for an hour –
nobody will know what occurred:
Yaris is covered (on the QT)

Soo's Tattoos – full 12-sign Zodiac encompassing her back
                    and the scenic Twin Peaks on her chest

Handsome Harris Holds court
~.~ being far nicer looking than
Any woman wishing his allegiance

'You Ever NOTICE
That Life is CA: Constant Audition
How Well Can YOU Interface?
In heaven, You'd better be Damn well-rehearsed!
\ \ \   \   \   \   \   \   \   \   \   \

In – http://tinyurl.com/lg7kfdz

Out – http://tinyurl.com/qc3nqkx

Warm Fuzzy BJ's –
So, since Sig met the special lady
he realizes he doesn't need Earth food anymore
'Just going to live on love and botanicals
~ ~

On a Stack of Scripts (not Bibles)

Bartenderess of Islands:
She'd make an ideal mother
the way she instinctively whisks away
Sig's camera's 'battery-in-charger' thingamajig
swiftly putting it into its crib (outlet) . . . .

Wisely, utilizing pre-set karmic guidelines
They have chosen Not to run that Kid program
but simply to entertain the earth people for 21 years
and Then they are Off to another world!

So? – There are Bigger events eclipsing the smaller ones

and When "The Sky Vision" hits us in the eye
We'll Know What to do and why

"True" Love – Usually when a man meets a woman
he wants to "do her" without further adieu
But – and This is a Big But –
when he's comfortably in the groove with her
He'll want to Save her (postpone the act
for about a month –
it Looks better on everybody's books)

Credits & Shout-Outs –

Brought To You By -- "Bill & Ted's Textellent Adventure"

When writer boy woke up this morning, he felt pretty dead
but after writing in style for awhile, he feels pretty energized
~ ~

Virginia Is For Lovers – And for Thinkers
Virgins are for Lovers – And for Tinkerers

Producer Extraordinaire –
Dylan Marko Bell: acute sense of timing
as on Tuesday the 6th Day of the Year
at 1999 North Alexandria
when he conversed with his star vehicle
now "Living The Life"

Top Spin bottom line – The Universe feels excellent
once you get a handle on
your constituent constellations
(performance & social skills)

Men's Pro Tennis Today . . .
Is a color coordinated fashion show
(Rafi in turquoise & orange shoes,
shorts, shirt & headband) with the
customary cross-court bullet shots
new Dick's Sporting Goods, Glendale CA

Scene 24: 'Call U on Fone from Harvard-Stone . . .

~.~ Adventure of the Month ~.~

a story dreamed up pretty quick
Selected DREAMS / SCENES

Harvard & Stone --
Night Owl band:

http://tinyurl.com/mrpgx2z

League Standings

Western

1. Ye Rustic Inn
2. Harvard & Stone
3. Scotland Yard – Canoga Park
4. Duke's – Malibu
5. HMS Bounty – Wilshire
6. Jamesons – Hollywood
7. Rusty Mullet –" next door
8. Pig 'N Whistle –
9. Crows Nest – Tujunga

10. Universal Bar & Grill –
11. BJ's – esp. Burbank
12. Black Angus – "
13. Islands – Glendale
14. 9 On Vine – at Fountain

15. Neptune's Net – P.C.H.
16. Nite Cap – San Francisco
17. Noc Noc – " " on Haight
18. Mario's – Shelter Cove
19. The Shanty – Eureka

Eastern

1. Newcomb's Ranch – Mt. Wilson
2. Lucille's SMOKEHOUSE
   BAR-B-QUE -- West Covina
3. Barnacles – Redlands
4. Hooz On 1st – Barstow
5. Wayside Inn – Mt. Shasta
6. Gold Room –   " CA
7. 1899 Bar & Grill – Flagstaff AZ
8. PJ's Village Pub – Sedona AZ

9. Kickers / Detour – Richfield UT
10. Silver Dollar Saloon – Leadville CO
11. Scarlet Tavern – across street "
12 Sabroso – Arroyo Seco NM
13. Slippery Noodle Inn – Indianapolis

14. Turn One – Nashville
15. Baja Sandbridge Virginia
16. The Heights – Broadway NYC
17. Lake Placid Pub & Brewery, NY
18. Margaritas –W. Lebanon NH

Harvard & Stone on Hollywood Blvd

bathroom in an old prison ship & Sarah Jean, Jennuin Hair Design, Tarzana CA

Part 2

Scene 25: A New Kind of Story . . .

. . . Told in Picto'grams
and mini-bites, thought capsules

There Is hope
at the end of the tunnel (lifetime)
                                    (~.~)
-------------------------------------{~.~}

Knowing two too perfect gals
Is a lot to contemplate –

Duality is a divine balance and
the best thing that can happen
'cuz you won't fall to either side
And it's always nice to have Back-Up:
i.e., Two cameras are better than one
(e.g., when one of them is hiding out)

Nice Feeling –
      when your camera lap dances into your laptop:
          uploads pics fast and clean (or 'quick & dirty')

Sigmond
Drinking the 'War Tire'–
Pronounced "war tar"
      "wahta" water
~ . ~ . ~ . ~ . ~ . ~ . ~

and Now Enjoy The Show . . . .

(e-Book link: 'Night Owl' band at Harvard & Stone)

http://tinyurl.com/kjhnow7

The 7 Sevens –
    7 Music Notes, 7 Chakras, 7 Sacraments, 7 Days
        7 Game Series, 7 Continents, 7 Rainbow Colors

Scene 26: A New Page = A New Stage

Just To Be Sure Your Hearts are Up & Running apace

We're going to start off with Two Numbers by one band:
   "TNT" and "Highway To Hell" "Watch Me Explode!"

Feeling the *Thrill* of new places: 1st grade school days ....
      The soggy wet winter coat closet, the puddly area
      with the drippy umbrellas, boots, rubbers & galoshes –
      and the square glass jars of peacock blue fountain pen ink
      on the wooden shelf at the bottom of the room-length window
      Sig has somewhat more To Say ....
      Well then, Aren't We ALL Lucky Today!!

Sigmond
Integrated Consciousnesses "I.C."

~ ~ ~ ~ ~ ~ ~ ~ ~ ~ ~ ~ ~ ~ ~ ~ ~ ~ ~ ~

See how many of these videos you can navigate:
tubing down the river YouTube (End of Tunnel & other videos)

http://tinyurl.com/n2mweop

Scene 27: Life IS a Movie . . .

Exhausting & THRILLING --

(Your) Life Is A Movie . . .
And Someday You'll See It In a Theater
~ ~

New 'chapterScenes' are Jumping Out in Both directions!

GOD <-> DOG MAD <-> DAM
    WAR <-> RAW {Chew your words thoroughly}

Immortality evolves in stages –
    1) early cognition
    2) medium development
    3) late stage: On Stage

Biological Expert mentation --

Billy Bob & Angelina
vs. Sigmond & Courtney House Outlaw
    wildly natural selection in the gene pool

Santa Has Just Arrived --
  and he Has your things:
    camera, wallet / $ / organics
      keys to get you back home and inside
        cel phone to fan your latest flame (~.~)

Poll figures –
Thrillary Cartoon and Can-Can Rice would "pole"
around Zero if allowed to perform in That arena

High On Life – Late At Night:

(e-Book link: Above Mt. Wilson)

http://tinyurl.com/q6cc3tm

Now Appearing --
In Herringbone – Houndstooth – Tattersall & Seersucker

For Your Textilicious Pleasure

Sigmond Professor of Theatrics
filled with On-Stage tricks
{Chew up the scenery thoughtfully}

above Mt. Wilson, Chilao CA & art imitates life: bird over bird

Scene 28: ~~ Imaginary Sushi & Such ~.~

Hold On, Everybody!
Aren't we all uber-Zooming through this Year!

Wasn't it just Christmas a little while ago?
And did we ascend right around Dec 21, 2012?

Can you Fathom what's Happening!
   while Sig gives 'Time' a speeding ticket

   ~ ~ ~ ~ ~ ~ ~ ~ ~ ~ ~ ~ ~ ~ ~ ~ ~ ~.~

Does THIS Ever Happen?
   You meet a person with whom you "Know"
   you've had warm conversations recently BUT –
   & here is another large But – you cannot recall
   where or when it was!! – Reincarnation reunion?
   or could you have met in a dream! or
   at the Rustic Inn or Wednesday BarBQs
   or Jumbo's or Gemini Manor ....
   It's a pleasant yet trippy feeling

On the same note –
   imaginary sushi place:
   according to memory bank *D*
   there's a tousled bushy-hair cutie
   at the far right end of the food bar
   (a scene from an assembled dream?)

Better Than a Dream –

LUX's Birthday Party: Wednesday at 9
at the universally beloved Jumbo's
~ musical gymnastica exotica ~
Ms. Lux is deeply gorgeous!
dark & (dare not say) delicious . . .

Other Power Dames: Reagan and Lily
Fancy Bottoms line: Be There Wednesday night!

Go by instinctive intuition
Or by intuitive instinct:
whichever floats your pineal gland
(but first flush the fluoride)

The Nice thing about nabinoids
is that they help you Live the dream
(morphing reality in an elevated mental state)

Pre-Production Enclave, Pre-Sunset

Began in Bel-Air on the 12th Day
of forever of heaven on Earth
P.S. #304: Sig ♥ U
P.S.2. Sage of Shasta:
And You Too!

Sincerely,

Sigmond 365 Day Santa

Dad & Mom & Dad likes to dance (at Gemini Manor)

Scene 29: Bangin' the Skeleton . . .

Dear Faithful Fans* --

We have NOT "Gone Off the Deep End" –
We are merely "Pushing the Envelope"

*Consideration –
  When too much information (TMI)
  gets 2B 2much 4U
  evaluate what to read now
  and what to save for later (or what to discard)

Now, Back "On Message:"
  re: Bangin' the Skeleton –
  "Don't Knock It 'til You've Boned It!"

People don't like it when someone gets Too confident –
  (it makes them feel like they're falling behind)

Sigmond respects people who get fired for
growing restless with workplace stagnation

It seems that much comedy today
stems from misshapen sexual encounters— and now
the growing stand-up usage of the female "V" word

Spandex on Steroids (original scene title)
Tattooed Mermaid

In Conjunction With Spiral Motion
          PRESENT

Tower of baby Babylon
  And adult Hollywood
  with KIM Anna Jasmine and J-me:
  high-flying skirt magic

"Almost" Off The Wall –
  Lady Bartenderess: can you squeeze the action hose
  while your special friend applies Siggy with needle ink

the way karma works –
 if you pout a lot
reality will slap you
 until you Snap Out of it

Go for The Best –
  Sage Apropos
  Sharp as a tack, cute as a button
  Sig suggests she & he consider working (entertaining) together

Lexi "engaging personality"–
  No need to get hitched
  but to keep charming us forever . . .

and continue writing your future
in your colorfully adventurous style

Without a doubt or hesitation
let's go to Boston
(symbol of American independence)

[character names will shift around
but our inclinations stay the course]
social navigator *Sigmond*
Powered by Chowder (New England)
and feeling his Quaker Oats

P.S. Comedy Is KIng –
    With a Jack off the Old Block
        & an Ace Joking with the Queen

favorite joke –
    "Do any of your relatives suffer from mental illness?"
    "No, they seem to ENJOY It" {~.~}

Experimental concept –
    When you're freshly in love
    everything seems a pleasure
    (as the endorphins circle playfully in your head)

last gasp for marriage –
    Is "tying the knot" roughly equivalent
    to tying a noose around the neck?
    (what u get when u stick ur neck out)

~ ~ ~ ~ ~ ~ ~ ~ ~ ~ ~ ~ ~ ~ ~ ~ ~ ~ ~

Hell's Bells – Open House:

http://tinyurl.com/ph3yur7

Bartenders: This Note's For You . . . .

(e-Book link: Lady Antebellum "Bartender")

http://tinyurl.com/pefqz4c

Now Everybody: Play awhile in the snack bar of life . . .

Fred 62 Freshwich & Aroma Café, Studio City CA

Scene 30: {~.~} Tonight's The Night – 15 Second Message

The Greatest Show On Earth
~ The Happiest Place Too ~
PRESENTS

Better Than A Dream --

LUX's Birthday Party: Wednesday at 9
~ musical gymnastica exotica ~
where extra cash is a handy asset

How Do We Love Thee?

Let us **Count** The Ways . . . .

Lux Luxuriously luscious Birthday Girl!

Fox Laser Eye awareness (X-ray vision)

Chelsea Sweet magnet of love
with heart-shaped derriere

Zeldah Legendof Alabama

Nixie Principal Lola

Topaz A Bright Gem

Ophelia Limber & Sensuous

Fiona Petite Nautilus

Gemini Twinkle Star

Reagan Fairy Tale Pretty

Rev Electric Rainbow Revolution

Delilah Cleopatra: vertical voluptuosity

Lily Classic Lovely strawberries & cream

Jacqui Holland Light Kiki Cheri

Ava Charlie Isa Jenna the iris

Priscilla Forever Young: always playful

Nataly Wood I Hope

Nadja Saucy Bartenderess & guitar goddess

Karen Grand Dame of Kindness

And handsome fellows Chase, Nick & Nate

Free Admission if you're on a mission
to fall in love (Off stage, Please)

Jumbos = Hot Chick City, esp. on Valentine's Day
(e.g., Skylar & her lady friends) – Once you've evolved to
high-flying social butterfly, marriage seems out-of-bounds

Sigmond
Observational Chameleon

When the feeling gets you –
   Fox, Sig wants to hug you So hard
   it's going to pull a muscle
      (not sure if it'll be his or yours)

Balance, Roll & Tone –
Wednesday Mornings on Sunny Grass:

http://tinyurl.com/od5c9mp

Brass Mermaid and the Beeswax Soaps

Scene 31: Life On Earth Is a . . .

. . Game of Experience –

and Our job as coaches
is to soften the learning pain

Letter to fellow planetarians
    We are Here to Do Shows:
        the art and essence of Living . . . .
the Nixie Principal
    teaches the how and who
        (the right way of things to do)

Nixie, Sig knows you see everything
            So he's become more careful
A Flowering of followers –
    Sigmond has a following
        (talker-stalkers with vim & vigor)

Sigmond Friend of Police & Gangstas Alike . . .
    that's how to swing the world together
    as Fox has a Trot
    and Barbara has a gene
    with which Sig would like to convene

Sigmond
Happy 2B Here

Cumbersome anagram: no pot pourri = pour it on or p

Scene 32: "Your 1st Time in Heaven?...

.. Well Then, Let's Help U get Adjusted!"
Nixie will check you in
(Nixie is our Principal, in principle)

AND we have the Threads
That will Fit you "to a T"...

You Know when newbies are arriving by Mustang
...when you hear those throat pipes Roar!

Mark Key D. Sod
& Artie Facial say -- Jumbo's Clown Kisses
     are cheesy / artificial
      but at least They're There!...

Then enjoy some sweet Asian pear
as you sit down low in the fuzzy chair

heaven is never finished
(it needs work)

Pairings –Real & Imagined
  Capri – March 15
  Siggy – February 14*

*the bride remains the variable
algebraically speaking

husband-in-training –
   action movies help a man
   come to know which breed of
   woman he'd like to blend with
   (a multi-faceted perspective)

P.S. Capri: Sig loves you
    for bringing your smart charm
    back to us (at the bar in the hood)
    As long as you are around
    Siggy will be a happy single

P.S.2 Dylan Filmmaker is moving Up & Out
    and Sig has a new (wi-fi) connection:
    "The Palermo Connection"

Religious Disclaimer --

(e-Book link: church electronic sign crawler)

http://tinyurl.com/ppy5efp

the photographer **&** 1739 Public House at Hollywood Blvd

1739 Public House beer menu **&** nacho burger & cocktail

"Getting it all Together" **&** Drawing Room on Hillhurst

Scene 33: "Herringbone Houndstooth Tattersall . . .

. . . Seersucker Corduroy & Burlap"

-- Attorneys of The Cloth –

Final Vinyl Flannels –
  Words love you – writers mend **Them**

Representing Elvis
Chuck Berry Sam Cooke Buddy Holly
  Little Richard Coasters Bobby Darin
Jerry Lee Lewis Everly Brothers Platters
  Dion & the Belmonts Tony Bennett
Sig Left his Heart in San Francisco --
and angelic virginity at Ye Rustic Inn

Tattooed Mermaid
    Proud To PRESENT

KIM – the best influence for Lexi
for reasons obvious and vampirical

Kick To the Finish –
  It took a guy 2/3 of a century to Learn
  What he was Born To Do! –
 To Write what's Right so it warms your heart too . . .

as will the singing voice of Marissa Hollenback

(Radiohead power ballad) http://tinyurl.com/p38gwec

Menu Says: "All Sandwiches Come With Fries"
          but do the fries orgasm as well? and If So,
     do they come all over the silly open-face sandwich? (~.~)
~ ~

Memory Is Telescopic –
  Looking back from 2015 –
  visualizers can see clearly to 1956
  in living color, e.g. Elvis' Golden Hits Vol. I
  (image of 12" gold record on red album cover)

  2009 seems like yesterday . . . and
  1995 is not much farther back, etc.
~ ~

Do's & Don'ts –
  Do drink all 9 innings (rounds)
    Don't burp in bartenders' faces

Sure, Sig did think about MJR every day –
but he also thinks about everyone else every day
(to keep the Universe in harmonic balance)

Sigmond
"Out There"

Patience Buehler
Countess of Pine Mountain Jenningsrealty.org

TRASH ONLY NO GARBAGE PLEASE

". . . And the Wisdom to Know the Difference!" &
Firecreek Coffee Company, Flagstaff AZ

Little Gateway & his big brother Toshiba & the long legs of the lawless

Scene 34: Back To Basics ->

Inexpensive food that will Also save you $ money
   by avoiding doctors and drugs –

Avocado Blue & Blackberries Broccoli sprouts Brown onions
Cucumber Dark chocolate Extra Virgin coconut & olive oils –
"They're SO Virgin, they've never even contemplated the Act!"
Garlic Ginger Green tea Organic apple juice Red wine
Sweet potato Tempeh Turmeric Walnuts Watercress Yogurt

These foods along with your daily
dose of sunlight Vitamin D (for better sleep)
and walking barefoot on (especially wet) grass or sand
(for healthful negative ions) will keep us from
illnesses of every kind (from colds to cancer)

You see, it's our microbiome / microflora (immune system)
   that keeps us healthy –
      Not the fancy-named & colorfully packaged,
         overpriced, risky (toxic) pharmaceuticals!

But Don't Tell the medical industrial complex –
because maintaining illness IS THEIR $ Lifeblood!
(we don't want too many homeless oncologists)

Sad but True
   as you likely already Knew

We now know that the (most profitable) #1 ruse
is statin drugs for cholesterol – even though
cholesterol is Not the problem – but we all fell for That
stinky pile (of disinformation) the medical media fed to us! . . .

http://tinyurl.com/ouf6tzk

Vaccinations are another Huge hoax –
 essentially a forced "pharma tax" on the sheeple
which WAS us until we wised up! . . .

http://tinyurl.com/o7jwu5p   articles.mercola.com/sites/ current.aspx

So, Stop feeding the beast for "sh!t" with built-in side effects
Or at best, they don't do Any Darn Thing at All . . .

& don't be afraid just because that's always been the norm –
We can do Without fear-based insurance:
When we pay for insurance, we are paying to Confirm
the conditioned fear ☹ that something bad may likely happen:
Don't Think That Way! Make your INTENTION that you'll be safe ☺

Sigmond's World of Super Peace
our new world is changing for the better:
we can all be "Healthy as a Horse"
(& done with the parasitic pharma industry)

[medical industry mantra – "If folks are misguided enough
          to come to us, then they'll be gullible enough
        to accept our 'treatments' "] http://tinyurl.com/nwfol6l

Modern Medicare: Part A: **A**maretto
  Part B: **B**oddingtons Part C: **C**uervo Part D: **D**ewar's

Humanity is an ambitious experiment – and humanitarianism
has moved ahead of the regal reptilians / underground cities

NOW Go Out And Have Some Fun
Every Friday night live music at the
free pool, low-cost beer, Big Fish Bar:

Sample of the Music:

http://tinyurl.com/khuy6t7

Scene 35: As Luck Would Have It . . .

. . . We would Have Luck as Well

Premier Verbal Projection

U can validate everything you do
If yoU aRe a crafty wordsmith . . .

Maybe it's Time 4U to Step Forward & Speak Up!

Snapshot In Time –
　Violet Ava Delilah Nadja Fox
　The Foxy Hearts Club:
　All Lovable at Once
　on any rainy or random day
　~ ~ ~ ~ ~ ~ ~ ~ ~ ~ ~ ~ ~ ~ ~ ~

Casual note to Sig's college roomie:
'looks like we'll be together forever . . . .

Look in the Fridge –
　every time you see that little bag
　of apricot kernels – eat 2 or 3 –
　so your cells maintain their normal growth
　and you grow strong as a hearty oak tree

With ALL his money –
  S Jobs didn't know this – because That's
  how Other rich businessmen Like it (because the
  medical industry thrives on disinformed sick people …
  and an olive oil-intensive diet is not the answer)

Medical school – legal drug dealer in**doc**trination school
  ~ - ~ - ~ - ~ - ~ - ~ - ~ - ~ - ~ - ~ - ~ - ~ - ~ - ~

Okay, Let's Get Back to the Fun Zone –
  which would be, of course,
  the inner sanctum of *gymnastica exotica*
  where the best time to shoot ur luv sparks
  is six or sevenish when the felines
  are in most need of attention
  (inquire within for deTails)

On That Note –
  The song "Magnet & Steel"
  is code for "muff & boner"
  but Which is more Poetic?

Speaking of Attraction –
  Ava: She has a bee-you-tee-full body of art
  and a sharp mind for lovin' too
  a totally non-dumb blonde (busty as well)

The Fox Factor: If you fall in love
                will you inform Sig
                or at least reform him. . . . . . .

Sig's just gonna Stay here at the lioness den
    until his little old heart goes out

Brain function note –
  less weed = more focal speed
  (but sometimes it's all we need)

Sigmond
Oxygen Rich

Sigmond's Word of the Day --

       narcheology: the study of ancient drugs

Scene 36: Crazy Like A Fox . . .

. . . Tall as a gazelle . . .

Scarlett Violet Magenta Macaroon
in skin-tight leopard-skin leotard
She & Sig get each other's goats
with a bit of playful ribbing

Violet keeps him on his toes –
as she is perfectly too much ...
Her birthday bash this year
at the magical age of 3 x 3 x 3
tops #22 at Good Luck bar

Top January 22nd Birthdays & Events –

Scarlett K Violet 1988
   gymnastica exotica
Linda Blair 'Exorcist' 1959
Jim Jarmusch 1953
   director: Night On Earth
Beverly Mitchell 1981
   TV: 7th Heaven
Michael Hutchence 'INXS' 1960-1997 😔
Steve Perry 'Journey' singer 1949
Sam Cooke 1935-1964
   "Chain Gang" singer
Bill Bixby 1934-1993
   TV: My Favorite Martian

John Hurt 'Elephant Man' 1940
1947 KTLA begins –
  1st TV station in Western U.S.
Ann Sothern 1909-2001
  TV: The Ann Sothern Show
D.W. Griffith 1875-1948
  director: The Birth of A Nation
Lord Byron 1788-1824
"Don Juan" poet, playwright,
  sexual escapades (see web link below)
Sir Francis Bacon 1561-1626
  lawyer-statesman-philosopher-scientist

http://www.biography.com/people/lord-byron-21124525#last-heroic-adventure
    or simply go to http://tinyurl.com/mk22kjp

Onward & Upward: **L**et's All Get There –
                    As Soon as we find the Right People
Who are also Super Aware (in their underwear)

This scene is dedicated to every man & woman
Who has ever frolicked at Jumbo's Clown Room . . .

Each time you go there –
This fountain of youth adds 1 day to your life
so, for Sig, that's about 1000 days
(having enjoyed its luster since 1991 –
thanks to location scout Mark)

Scene 37: Life = More than beer, tacos & tatas . . .

. . . but not Much more!

Club 31/30:
  KIM   Allie J
  Daesha   Mars Indiana

  Dylan M Bell   Lexi Bee
  Geoffrey Whittaker   Katy Perky . . .

These are Sig's favorite characters – and
"A Team of Wild Horses Couldn't Tear Us Apart"
  to quote Elvis' strong song "Stuck On You"

Consummation of hot snacks:
  burgers, beef or chicken sliders

Nothing is quite as pleasurable
as nibbling the flesh of a fresh lime
and other sensuous organic tissues

Saidman Said –

  "Count me In at Ye Rustic Inn" (sliders photo below)
    with his able entourage of Ojai troubadours

Having an active, avid listener is
the joy of an eager, intense talker

Evolving wisdom – the better you feel about yourself
   the more attractive others appear to be

May You have a happily busy artistic life

Sig wishes you all a boatload
of beer, tacos & sexy sliders—
the Basic Building Blocks of Life
///////////////~·~\\\\\\\\\\\\\\\\

Too Many e-Mails in your inBox?
   U have 3 choices:
      a) delete (escape)   **b)** save for later   **c)** savor now (& forever)

This page is full – Go in Peace
   (The Mass has Ended -- but the best of our lives is just Beginning)

beef or chicken sliders, Ye Rustic Inn

Scene 38: The Future Has Already Happened . . .

. . . even if you Think you can alter the future
    by making last-minute decisions / changes –
    You are just conforming to the future as
    it already shall have been [future perfect]

The Dark Side – If you have the misfortune to watch
                  or read the everyday world news
                  you'll see that adults (& nations) behave

                  Far Worse than the most unruly children*

    and the more their obscene wealth torments them,
    the more likely they are to bomb, brainwash & poison us
    (e.g., charging more than our life savings for chemo and
    radiation {destroying our bodies For Profit} – Instead of kindly
    asking us to eat apricot kernels every day – 'cuz
    There's No Damn Money to Be Made selling apricot seeds!)
    Go Figure.

*Not That Much Difference . . .
    between a baby's frantic, helpless Outburst of Crying and an

    adult's accusatory, fault-finding, noise making horn-honking!
    (it's not a fender bender – just a bruised ego)

Push Back – Don't let the gubmint bully you around
They work for us (allegedly):
Turning Right at a red light – with No traffic in sight
(Where there is usually a coordinated Green Arrow!)
is No reason to send $585 to heartless, money grubbing,
robot camera-dependent, exploitative institutions,
e.g., Ventana County of sheeple

The Bright Side – Sigmond's creative / social life is like wildfire
spreading quickly and gathering momentum:
Look for an eventful national splash

Right Now –> Go Ahead –> Enjoy the Show: (Big Fish band & other videos)

http://tinyurl.com/mxzzcnh

Sigmond
"Johnny Apricotseed"
Man of the People
Mountain Hiking Guide: Mt. Wilson, Mt. Shasta, Humphreys Peak (AZ)

looking at Mt. Baldy from Mt. Wilson **&** Flagstaff AZ

panoramic city of angels: from Mt. Wilson CA

One of the Very Best: MLK Jr

Scene 39: Room for Improvement . . .

Out with the old and IN with the New!

"If it IS broken, DO Fix It!

When there's a hurdle in your path
Jump Over It
if you can't wiggle around it

Inside story –
    When we feel pain (from stress)
    That's a sign we're in a mess –
    And when we feel sick
    There are actions to take
    That will do the trick . . .

When you find a problem area
"Get Down On It" and Work Out with it
Don't let it cramp your style:
Iron out the kinks— OR Toss It
and create something more useful

Rise to a higher level –
    Stay on top of your board
    and when you're on a low wave
    be ready to climb onto a higher one
    where you'll move faster and farther

as you process your art

Ovation Inn (innovation) PRESENTS:

Things are Not THAT certain – So, every time you blurt out the
token Power Word **"A**b-So-**LUTE**-ly"
you must do a shot of **V**odka

and if you're feeling mighty, drink a "ton" of it –
Ton the tiny monster word broadcasters love to throw around

Sigmond's Word of the Evening --
horchata – a chatty hooker

~ ~

"with Arms Wide Open" & Big Mama's
& Papa's pizzeria wall, Hollywood Blvd

Los Feliz, Vista and Village Theatres & French onion soup, Dresden
vintagecinemas.com   near Hollywood Blvd

Scene 40: Invention laboratory

& seasonal readjustment substation

mAtt caRpenTer photo at Electric Daisy Carnival 2009

P.S. Self-analysis (and writing
    your best understanding of it)
    is a most satisfactory therapy

Helios thru the Yellow Umbrellawear at Fred 62

twin dandies **&** Joan Dandelion

camera man **&** Mt. Lowe / San Gabriel Peak CA July 2014

Barney Tower & Saidman   **&**   the mane lion Saidman Said
Deer Leg bluesy country rock   **&**   leader of the band Deer Leg

Scene 41: 'Love This Life, Love These People . . .

"Where Too Much Is Never Enough"

Starring Ye Jumbo's Clown Room* -- *gymnastica exotica:*

where they serve you 'square meals'
     in the form of rounds (of drinks)

Yvonna Fox Lily Lola Caroline Fiona Jacqui Zeldah Zoe
Nixie Lux Priscilla Magilla Ava Simone – with Nadja
Barbara Liane Michelle Kristina Chase Nick & Nate

You'll come for the ladies but Stay for the Music
and the fraternal camaraderie (brotherly love)

Rustic Inn – Starring Lexi Kim Caitlin Allie Sam
              Anna Jasmine Daesha Deja Carly Lanier
              Guy ("ghee") Russell Lehr Igor Paul
              Gordon Jordan Karen Susan Harris

Fred 62 – Jessica Erin Corey Erin2

1739 Public House – Alona Monet Courtney Izzy

Palermo – Michelle Beata Heather

Deer Lodge (Ojai) –
Saidman Said Kat Monica Robin
Jeff Ariel Don-Lee Bear Tom Scott

*Life Is a Dance & A Balancing Act
Have Your Chakras Spin-Balanced

For Serendipity, Simpatico & Synergy

Sigmond
Not a Processed Food –
But a Processed Entertainer

Bottoms Up line:

Drink to Your Heart's Content (~.~) or at Least until You "Break the Seal"

Scene 42: (~.~) Enchanting Face, Deep Fox Eyes . . .

"What's Going On" – Marvin Gaye queries . . .

   well THIS Is –
Daesha
Svetlana
Sam-antha
& Rachel   http://RachelsCosmicCuisine.com

The results are Emotional Fluency for a watery Pisces

Sigmond needs to learn – cute waitresses-servers are not
                  just sparkly bulbs on a Christmas tree

Reality of experience – Sig will probably end up with himself
             'cuz he's not so sure about the rest of you

"weirdness" is the spark of creativity
~~~~~~~~~~~~~~~~~~~~~~~~~~

Sig just climbed his way
Back Up to Six (6) Feet Under
due to creatively risque comments . . .

but when he told her
he loves her diction
she raised him straight up
out of the writers' grave

so at this Point
Sig's going to OBEY himself:
That is, Behave himself

Awe-Right! That's Enough of a warm-Up!
   for the new radio drama:
      "Rhonda's Romantic Dinners"

Men call in to report suspected 'cheating'
by their partners. Then the ladies are offered a
romantic dinner for two— and they tell "Rhonda"
-- played by dynamic Daesha – with whom
they would like to have the dinner –
and we discover whom the woman is courting.
A gender reversal of "Ryan's Roses" on KIIS-FM

Wisdom dropping –
   Maintaining your creative momentum is
   More important than the size of your audience

How "love" works:
   You don't Try to make a relationship happen –
   The Forces of (compatible) Natures Try YOU
   and measure how You Handle It

Sigmond
Graduate Rainman
(Full-Scale Entertainer)   (e-Book link: Blue Flame of Amour)

http://tinyurl.com/og6xdxj

Amy Jones singer
Ultra massage therapist

   &   Andrew performing at Brewgrass, Weed CA

nice slice at Fred 62   **&**   bathroom at nucleus of the universe

Scene 43: You can Drive in your Dreams . . .

    Gliding along the guiding, glowing double Day-Glo
    Bright as Electric orange centerline road reflectors . . .
    weaving left & right like a rollercoaster up & down
    for a fast-paced viewing-in-motion pleasure

Sigmond Chatterbox
pushing the boundaries of civility:
the speculative lust to communicate –
once known as "Love with the Proper Stranger"

art space – individual or group

{black or color pencils, pens or paints}

Let your dreams be your guide

Scene 44: "Anatomy of A Dinner Plate" – 4 Photos . . .

Affordable Culinary Excellence –
　　Start with #79 Tiger Cry $10.95
　　　　at Hollywood Thai 5241 Hollywood
　　　　　　half block west of Harvard & Stone
　　　　　　one block west of Jumbo's Gymnastica Exotica

Are you ever "too early" or simply "twirly"–
　　Words are meant to dance for you

Image Control – pre-judgments about a person can only continue if
　　the person does nothing to counter-program those perceptions

Hollywood Thai on Hollywood Blvd

Scene 45: Don't JUST Count Ur Blessings . . .

. . . ORGANIZE Them
    into a Cohesive Unit . . .

Without getting too flowery –
the reason Sig Wants to live forever
Is that he HAS To (It's Not a choice)
but he is pleased to live forever
with his teachers David Wilcock (gaiamtv.com)
Dr. J. Mercola (everything health: Mercola.com)
Ed Snowden c/o Glenn Greenwald 'Guardian'
George Carlin, Bill Hicks, Dave L & Jerry Seinfeld
Chad Benson: KXNT-AM, Las Vegas
  Coast To Coast AM: George John, Ken & Shannon: KFI-AM 640
And able handlers Michael and Dylan of New Jersey
Adam of Bel-Air (& Inglewood), Geoffrey of NAU-Flagstaff
Tobias of Canada and Kendra of DT-LA

  plus (+) sketch comedy writing partners Ty & Daesha

Amber of Silver Lake, Eliza of Santa Fe
Jim Noelle & Michael in the Green Mountain State of Vermont

If YOUR NAME (is not) HERE
  please Scream at the script keeper
    im-MEDia-ate-Lee!

Pushing the Agenda –
  The author began writing an
  "On-the-Town social lifestyle" narrative / column
  on December 9 – 51 days later:

  we're at scene #45 . . . Read On! . . .

Columning is like other top pleasures—
once you're in the groove & Up to speed
  you can do it 2x/day, w/o missing a beat
~ . ~ . ~ . ~ . ~ . ~ . ~ . ~ . ~ . ~ . ~

Sig's Pledge to You –
  If You Ever need (want) to Know
  Anything about Anything
  Sail your request to him

  and he will GOOGLE* IT

  *more Knowledge than GOD & our parents Combined!

God is Out on His meal break ...

But Someone needs to Say:
  "LIVE From L.A: It's another Sunny Day!"

Scene 46: Painting the Floor With one Foot . . .

. . . Beer spill is the 'paint' to be spread evenly . . .
     It's Not That Hard To Do

Once your habits become obvious to you
You can manage/enjoy them all the "bettermore"

Lately, many are steadily following impulses
that they're pleased to have actually developed

You Don't Have To Read the Cliff Notes
To Know that Life Is A Party for your Eyes
and tobacco can't help you on That one

Club 22 –
is less about bullets (of stupid)
& more about arrows (of cupid)

Put THIS in your pipe & Smoke It!
The major thing to absorb from *cannabis herbicus*
is that "we can learn to accept things that are helpful to us –
the fleeting 'paranoia' is just a defensive reaction of
rejection of validating our acquiring a benign addiction"

Looking for a dinner tip?
Ask for the marbled beef or
the articulated mahi mahi (dolphin)

Sigmond walking a tightrope between
hapless schmuck & Carlin esque orator

Allow him to warm Your heart and musically
vibrate your eardrums >(~.~)< (e-Book: Fire Flames powered by gas)

http://tinyurl.com/qboajpr

Harvard & Stone on Hollywood Blvd

Harvard & Stone: front bar **&** delightful light

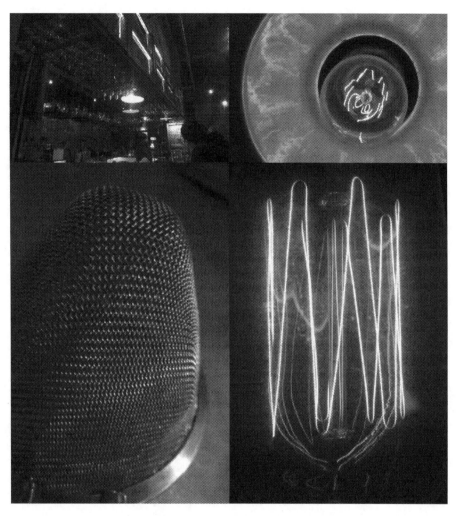

not a microphone **&** sexy filament

Scene 47: 4 Photos {&} Not A Pixel More!

If a man thinks he doesn't want to "do it"
   he is not being honest with himself . . .

And as if the squeezy full-body hugs
are just for polite (social) purposes
~ ~ ~ ~ ~ ~ ~ ~ ~ ~ ~ ~ ~ ~ ~ ~ ~ ~ ~

No sports coverage here
Only Real issues that make
You Hot (steamy tissues)

Always Watching your State of Addiction
(A State for which Sigmond Cares)

Sigmond "ISO 3200 Vivid"
Engaging Everyone and
Therefore Marrying No 1

Sometimes the best things are right under our noses
or on your desktop: Malwarebytes is the one to use
to help the laptop stop acting like a belligerent child –
which happens all too often

Edited Out (or in?) -- Cursing the Cursor:
   'ever wonder why the tiny white arrow on your
   laptop screen is called a "cursor"–
   It's 'cuz when it 'freezes' or "goes AWOL"
   All you can Do is Curse At It!
   and the f'n F5 function key doesn't help either:

when it's all in Super Slo-Mo mode . . .
We thought these little computers are
supposed to Help us – NOT fook with our Heads!
Sometimes you just want to scream "BOA SHIT!"
(see page 6 of *Twayne's Mental Cookbook*)

It's nice to have a best influence
from whom Sig has learned not only
about talking too much/often – but about
not sending messages before they are due

e.g., February (Mystic Hot Springs Utah)

You can let your meat loaf . . .

. . . at Ye Rustic Inn

Scene 48: Middle-aged Ladies Need Love Too . . .

. . . "dirty old men" are fairly irrelevant

Pairs & Triplets –
"Feel Like Makin' Love" Bad Co. And
"Sexual Healing" Marvin Gaye
Justin Selleck And Tom Timberlake

"Freebird" over a "Stairway To Heaven" on top "Hotel California"
(and there are many more combos in *Twayne's Mental Cookbook*)

Looking for the smartest LAdy in the LAnd –
maybe it's the future doctor who wrote
her e-mail address on Sig's note paper
in exactly the right place

Club 30 over Club 22—

Lexi, Allie, Daesha Deja Hillary KIM, Stefanie

A magnificent seven to fill up the week
& Hillary eyes: too sly for ordinary guys

Endless Grunge coming your way
Daesha well-sculpted face, Sig luvs her ex-
pressions of everything (facial smartness)

Best course of human discourse is intercourse
That is, no matter what things we do or say
Writing is not as poignant as a roll in the hay

Tonight might go on forever
Let's agree we're on the right track
which need not include . . .

Watching an NBA game on TV
or watching ice freeze or
hockey or soccer –
video games: more adventuresome

Sigmond still likes to sell Baseball,
fascinated by the high-speed geometry
of the ball blasting (or skidding) off the bat
in a high-reaching 3-dimensional visual spectacle
    \o oo ooo oooo ooooo oooooo ooooooo!

Sport of Life – flagrant freedom bugs the heck
                    out of the average employee at work

After work, go to heaven – an acquired acquisition –
You'll "Know It" when you arrive (at Ye Rustic Inn)
where you can let your meat loaf and eat it too
Sigmond
Drink salesman at point of purchase,
engaging conversations at Ye Rustic Inn

Romantic couples videos at lowball prices
e.g., Susie & Lauren

Much Appreciation:
Sig is Not Glenn Greenwald but he sure loves that man like a Guardian angel

Stefanie bartenderess at Birds on Franklin **&** Red & white hot Camaro
on the outskirts of Hollywood

200 mph Z 28 **&** modern Thunderbird creampuff

The Climax

Scene 49: Match.com & Snatch.com Join Forces To . . .

. . . . . . **Proudly PRESENT:**

Perky & Sigmond

Dear perky Superbowl Torch Singer:
    Sigmond thinks Rugrat Brand is okay but now it's Time to
    Step Up to the Plate & Hit an allegorical metaphorical Home Run!

Not just because Siggy respects such an accomplished career
but because he wants to be affiliated with that magic!
4 hours sleep is enuff: 'cuz we've got Places to Go & Things to Do!

https://en.wikipedia.org/wiki/The_Prismatic_World_Tour

Sig saw a bevy of adoring Day-Glo cobalt blue
   and fuchsia pink hair-adorned fans
     at a Staples Center show

Sigmond
Mountain Hiking Guide: Mt. Wilson, Mt. Shasta, Humphreys Peak (AZ)

and on top of L.A: 10,064' http://tinyurl.com/k9ohdut . . . . .

Photo-Videographer:
shooting a music video of virtuoso rock band 'Mothership' –
starting with a 2 hour 20 minute DVD of their show Saturday Night
at '9 On Vine' (which WON'T be on You Tube)

(~.~) HAPPY VALENTINE'S MONTH
~~~~~~~~~~~~~~~~~~~~~

[This proclamation was sent to more than 100 e-Witnesses]

moon with atmosphere & It's All Downhill from Here!

view from Mt. Baldy, above Upland CA & author's house

Scene 50: As Time Speeds Ahead . . .

Deeper and more eternal than tattoos
(file under "Itemization of Skills")

1) Rock Concert DVD   "Mothership" on Route 66
2) Colorful photo-video to
    Perky Valentine   "6 photos + YouTube Channel Sigmond"

3) meeting Rachel   "Biola philosophy"
    at 8K' hiking back from the top of L.A.'s
    tallest peak, above Upland, CA (see video link: p. 177)
4) Regional Food Bank   "donations needed / accepted"
    Box 268988 Oklahoma City
5) Jumbo's Gymnastica Exotica Dinner Theater **(3rd line of p. 153)**
    "45 high-performance bio-machines"

How Is Time Treating YOU?!
    It was pretty easy for Sig to go from 2014 to 2015
    but these new months are flying by even faster
        "Holy Rocket Sled, Batman!"

When Time Goes THIS Fast
It's hard Not to enjoy the ride!
because we are all creating a style bigger than life!
and THAT is the core of human sanity (mental sanitation)

Sigmond
Spewing philosophy Again
as a well-behaved actor

Sigmond is doing 66 in March: Route 66 at 100
and 140 on Auto Club Speedway with 'Mothership'
    virtuoso guitarist Courtney +2

The way we Behave is by choosing whose space
we give more consideration – sometimes it's a
close decision but a choice must be made
(e.g., which way to reach to pluck a few sugar packets)

Fred 62 on a wet fog night at 12:30 AM Wednesday
is society at its highest (people high on socializing)

"Which is better: the bacon or the big round waffle?
    It's a philosophical question – or rhetorical question –
    take as much time as you need"

Sleeping with Europe –
    Generally, people over there sleep from 2 to 8 AM –
    Sig is shifted 8 time zones ahead – sleeping 6 PM to 12 AM (Pacific) –
    and up when people both here And There are Up 'n At It!

The Big Tour –
Europe & Asia: Feb-May (e-Book link: Prismatic Vevo Tour)

    http://tinyurl.com/mgptm5n

Magic 7 Firework: "Wide Awake: Teenage Dream
                E.T: The One That Got Away: Last Friday Night
                Part of Me: Dark Horse"

30 yr old Scorpio with a classic movie star face
and a Kick-ass 53 week Concert Schedule!

As *A Soap Opera Is Born* (Scene 1),
50 Scenes in 58 days was born on Dec 9, 2014
with the *L.A. Weekly* as the prime target . . .
On Feb 3, 2015, it is *Match.com* (Scene 49)
with a Super singer as honorary subject

As long as Sig is alive (sporting an Earth body)
You will all be privy to current updates . . .

To Sugar or Not To Sugar –
   Sig has very little taste for sugar nowadays
   and That really frustrates cancer gremlins:
   so they starve and he goes On! (without them)

OK, Enough Happy News!

Here is today's Video Feed –
   fodder for the Artistic Mind:

(e-Book link: "Walk / Don't Walk" signal)

http://tinyurl.com/q4ntffu

Regional Food Bank of Oklahoma

The author hereby expresses his appreciation for the computers, printers and Ben at Copymat on Sunset Boulevard, photowork Michael Perrick, Cyber Jim, Microsoft (Word 2013, Wireless 800 Desktop & Internet Explorer)

and to Apple (Safari) for seeing a Toshiba Satellite* drift away
before its first birthday (into an unresponsive coma with Alzheimer's)

The laptop was a major source of psychological mayhem
and a goldmine of writing material . . .

Don't mortgage your soul for a flicker of hope:
Know When to let go – of a person, a computer,
a poker hand or anything else that "loyalty to" is
only self-sabotage – that is, don't trust something
that is suspiciously untrustworthy

[When you're not sure what you're dealing with
don't stick your drive into it]

*happy ending – After running CClean (cnet.com)
   the Satellite returned to normal, quick & efficient operation

And finally, no matter how far out your life gets –
the kind folks at Jumbo's will bring you back to Earth
~ ~

The last page "tailgate party"

At 11:18 AM on 2-14-15, Sig went silent:
To the great Joy and Relief of Everyone . . . .
& Then he went into full-on professional grade monologue

Potentiality – when $J = 18$, $S = 80$ . . . . . . 8s are Wild,
   legal and Totally copacetic, one might add

"There's a time and a place for everything" but some of
   us may have Neither! – Not a reason for self-deprecation
   (Unless one needs to deprecate all over oneself)

Here's a "great idea" –
   To Keep the home team fans Happy:
   The Home Team Always Wins
   (or the other team isn't invited back!)

BEEF & pea BOWL

The **Mid-West**	vs.	The **Middle East**
(Higher states)		(Uri Nations)

Illinois	Greece
Ohio	Egypt
Michigan	Turkey
Minnesota	Persia (from which Iran)

On the Stadium SONY Sound System:

Set the Volume at 10

the 1k Hertz band at +2

300 Hz and 3k Hz at -2

100 Hz and 10k Hz at -10

"The Flying V"

But for some bands: AC/DC

You can turn everything up to the ZZ Top!

~ ~

~ ~ ~ ~ ~ ~ ~ ~ ~ ~ ~ ~ ~ ~ ~ ~ ~ ~ ~ ~

Preachers with **melodramatic diction** –

"Scottish vowel stretchers"

Instead of saying 'God' ("Godd")

They wail out 'Gawd!' **("Gaw-awd!")**

With that **profound creepy tone of authority**

Closing Act –

In zebra spots and leopard stripes
     Siggy & Deep hopCar
       go "Hand-in-Hoof"

We will always love JbeeFKake
  Winterspring Summerfall

Sigmond
Stem cell of consciousness
Sporting the V 7.1 vinyl heart

The Downside:
  Sig's left brain Left and his right brain Ain't

Guten Nacht and *Buenos Noches!*
  (gluten not in our nachos)

Two songs for the road –

A heart tugger by Ed Sheeran

http://tinyurl.com/lbsyytv

a solid rocker by Def Lepperd

http://tinyurl.com/q67yb3o

sonic wave generator

1st Viewers: Brandon at the Melody, John at The Fox and Hounds and
Kari & Matt at Coffee Cartel all love "50 Scenes in 58 days"
And all the Interactive web links!

network affiliates

Jim & Noelle – New England . . . . . Billy Joe Daniel – Virginia
Dena Walker – Nashville . . . . RiYeN rOoTs – Asheville NC . . . . .

Byron Strolberg – Greenville NC
Mary Ried – Chicago
Bob Botto – Houston-Baytown

Chloe S Atlantis – Dubai

Eliza & Betsy – New Mexico
Douglas Lipper – Colorado
Mystic Mike – Utah
Gerald & Geoffrey – Arizona

Mark Fargo & Zack – Area 818
Gus Hudson – Highland Park-Echo Park
Tobias & Angela – Hollywood
Adam R. Singer – Santa Monica-Venice
Saidman Said – Ventura-Santa Barbara
Lisa Robinson – Shell Beach & Apple Valley
Tory, Alicia, Whitney & Co.– San Luis Obispo
Kristopher Wayside Sage of Mt. Shasta

About the Author

Author Twayne, photo-videographer, mountain hiking guide
& health advocate, has a bachelor's degree in business/accounting
from Arizona State University. He has published the witty 'encyclopedia'
Twayne's Mental Cookbook and hosted a Time-Warner cable TV talk
show. From New York, he lives in L.A., with friends in Mt. Shasta,
Flagstaff, Santa Fe, Asheville NC, Virginia, Vermont . . .

Index